IT TAKES A ~~VILLAGE~~ CAMPUS

15 INITIATIVES TO IMPROVE RETENTION

BY KYLE ELLIS, PH.D.
FOREWORD BY JOE CUSEO, PH.D.

ISBN: 978-1-936946-90-7

The Nautilus Publishing Company
426 S Lamar Blvd., Suite 16
Oxford, MS 38655
Tel: 662-513-0159
www.nautiluspublishing.com

First Edition

Front cover design by Wil Oakes
Interior design by Sinclair Rishel

Printed in USA

10 9 8 7 6 5 4 3 2 1

CONTENTS

FOREWORD

I am honored to write this foreword to Kyle Ellis' book, *It Takes a Campus*. In 2010, I made a visit to Ole Miss to provide professional development on enhancing the first-year experience and promoting student success. When I arrived, I was amazed to find a first-year experience program that was designed, administered, and delivered almost entirely by volunteers--including the program coordinator, course instructors, and peer mentors. I was stunned to find such a sizable portion of the campus community so dedicated to promoting student success and so willing to invest such substantial amounts of personal time to the program with little or no formal compensation.

When I made a return professional development visit to Ole Miss in the fall of 2015, I was pleased to discover that the university's fiscal and logistical support for student success programming increased dramatically. What the volunteer force of student-success advocates at Ole Miss did was pour passion and unselfish commitment into a modest, fledgling program, carefully collected hard data on the program's positive impact on student retention, intentionally showcased the data to key campus leaders, and persuaded the university to do the right thing: Make a data-driven decision to scale up the program so it could exert a more systemic and sustained effect on the student body.

It Takes a Campus captures the Ole Miss' success story in detailed, step-by-step fashion so that its success might be replicated on other campuses. It provides a planning blueprint and a procedural template that readers can use to learn from the Ole Miss experience to build a successful retention program on their own campus—without having to "reinvent the wheel." What distinguishes this book from other publications—and enables it to fill a void in the extant literature on student retention—is its highly practical, actionable focus. Other books on student retention start with theories and attempt to tease out their implications for practice; this book starts with hands-on practices that are clearly identifiable and immediately applicable. More than merely a "show-and-tell" success story, this is truly a practitioner's guide for creating an effective campus-wide retention program. It provides honest, blow-by-blow description of what worked effectively from the get go, as well as mistakes made and lessons learned from those mistakes. The book is infused with thought-provoking questions that prompt readers to reflect on and implement action-oriented strategies for replicating effective practices adopted at Ole Miss and for circumnavigating obstacles Ole Miss encountered along its journey toward full-scale implementation of a successful retention program.

What makes the Ole Miss story particularly powerful is that it took place at a flagship research university. Unlike other universities of its Carnegie type, the University of Mississippi didn't attempt to redress the retention-and-completion challenge by simply elevating its admissions standards and excluding students with lower levels of academic preparedness. Instead, Ole Miss maintained its historic commitment to access and inclusivity by continuing to admit and educate academically "at risk" students, including a substantial number of students from underrepresented ethnic and socioeconomic backgrounds. Given the diversity of students served by Ole Miss, the significant impact its retention efforts have had on student success, and the comparatively short amount of time it took to generate this impact, the practices described in this book warrant careful examination and potential emulation by other colleges and universities across the country.

Joe Cuseo

Ole Miss takes retention effort seriously, and numbers prove it

Tom Eppes

GUEST COLUMNIST

The cost of higher education is becoming an issue in the presidential campaign, with candidates generally agreeing on two points: High cost makes a college education inaccessible to lower-income Americans who need a diploma to advance up the economic ladder. And those who have access to loans are left with staggering debt. An estimated eight million people are now in student loan default, and many more struggle each month to make payments.

A third problem doesn't earn as much attention — the devastating effect of debt on students who drop out before earning a diploma, either because they were poorly prepared for college or ran headlong into health issues, family issues or another tough life experience. Their loans aren't forgiven, but their lack of a diploma can have an enormous impact on their ability to make payments.

Is there an answer? Yes: A focused, all-hands-on-deck commitment to student success without reducing one bit of the rigor of a leading academic institution. Retention is a term universities use to measure student success, tracking their progress one semester at a time until graduation. A key marker for comparing student success at different universities is freshmen retention, which reports how many freshmen were still enrolled during the fall semester of their second year.

For the elite private universities who pride themselves on the number of applications rejected and the quality of students admitted, the freshmen retention rates are extraordinary. Columbia and Yale report 99 percent freshmen retention, and other "Ivies"

hang close with 97-98 percent. Percentages are similar for the Honors College at the University of Mississippi, which achieved 97.8 percent retention in the 2013-2014 year.

Viewed more broadly, the University of Mississippi's overall retention rate doesn't look as good, but it's remarkable nonetheless. Ole Miss is the retention leader among the state's public universities, setting an all-time record of 86.5 percent retention for the 2015-16 academic year. That's more than 10 points away from the elite private universities, but it's an enormous achievement other public universities are sending representatives to Oxford to study.

Why is 86.5 percent a good number? Consider the differences between the elite freshmen classes at Harvard, Princeton and public flagships in Virginia and North Carolina. They have become prestigious at least partly through exclusivity, accepting only the highest performers. In Mississippi, exclusivity is flipped on its head. In fact, all public universities here accept any resident with an ACT score of 16 and a class GPA of 2.5. That's considered by ACT experts to be the very minimum standard for college success. Some describe that policy as "open enrollment," meaning just about anybody with the desire can enroll. It's a noble policy for America's poorest state to offer opportunity for everyone, but it creates an extraordinary challenge for universities to help under-prepared students succeed in a rigorous academic setting.

How has Mississippi's flagship university become a retention leader, even in that environment? As with any complex challenge, there is no single answer. But it starts with a passionate commitment from the top.

A retention culture gained real momentum in the past six years at Ole Miss as almost every campus school and department joined the retention initiative through various programs and under the leadership of a Retention Advisory Board representing 16

departments and supervised closely by former provost and now acting Chancellor Morris Stocks.

New methods for improving retention are constantly tested, but just a few of the biggest contributors include:

» A first semester class that teaches new students how to be successful in college (now includes 80 percent of non-Honors College students);

» FastTrack, which accepts about 10 percent of freshmen into a program with smaller classes and selected professors who commit to broader student engagement and mentoring;

» A Center for Student Success that monitors grades and reaches out to struggling students with personal advisers;

» Detailed daily reporting that arrives in 36 inboxes every morning with retention information sorted by gender, ethnicity, residency and even retention data within each school (Accountancy, Applied Sciences, Business, Education, Engineering, Liberal Arts, Pharmacy, Journalism and General Studies);

» More than 250 clubs that offer every student an opportunity to engage with others, and feel at home more quickly;

» The Luckyday Scholarship, which offers financial aid as well as tutoring/counseling, required study hall and social events that help form a Luckyday culture;

» And one unofficial contributor to success: Reporting retention data by school has created friendly competition between the deans for improved retention in the schools they lead.

Student success requires a personal commitment to every single student, a difficult challenge in a large university but the best answer to improved retention, student success and better lives for more people.

Tom Eppes is chief communications officer at the University of Mississippi. Contact him at teppes@olemiss.edu.

INTRODUCTION

"Retention" is a buzzword frequently used by higher education practitioners. Many professionals working at institutions of higher learning focus on retention, are directly involved in retention efforts, or are accustomed to hearing their colleagues grumble about the need to improve retention rates. Retention rates, specifically, for first-time, full-time (FTFT) freshmen, are very important. Such percentages are good indicators of institutions' potential six-year graduation rates, which are factored into national rankings, and serve as a key component of school budgets—the more students are retained, the more tuition dollars institutions collect. With much emphasis being placed on retention rates, one would think colleges and universities would have it figured out by now. Unfortunately, this is not the case. In today's post-secondary environments, where a record retention rate is applauded one day, only to be followed by directives to improve the ratio the following year, will there ever be an end to the retention madness? Probably not. However, rather than getting too excited or stressed about good or gloomy years, respectively, I encourage campus professionals, who are involved in retention efforts, to keep pushing ahead in the name of student success, satisfaction, and persistence.

When I began working at the University of Mississippi in 2004 as an academic advisor, the word "retention" was not in my daily vocabulary. The desire to advise students was my primary purpose for coming to work each day. Fast-forward 11 years, and many days, I feel as if my sole purpose for being here is to ensure that our retention rate continues to increase. A lot has happened in those 11 years. From working on the academic side of university athletics and becoming an administrator to earning a doctorate and overseeing a student success center that currently employs 35 campus professionals who work daily to make sure our students are successful, I feel well prepared to lead our institution's retention efforts. Although I no longer have the opportunity to work with individual students as much as I would like, I understand the importance of the greater good that my position can accomplish. Managing a tremendous staff of caring campus professionals, who are at the core of our retention efforts, is a responsibility I do not take lightly. Even though it is not easy, and some days, months, and even years are better than others, I fully embrace both the good and the bad times on this ride we call student retention in higher education. On a completely related note…I enjoy the good times the best!

It Takes A Campus takes readers on a journey of my experience from a novice in retention efforts to a campus leader in the field of student retention. I will be the first to admit that I do not have all the answers. However, based on my education, experience, and continued growth in the profession, I feel confident that the fruits of our retention efforts and our FTFT freshman cohort persistence rates reflect the positive impact we are making. In 2008, when the University began to take action on our FTFT retention rate (78.3%), little did I know that agreeing to serve on a large retention committee would propel me to where I am today. With our recent retention record-setting year (86.5%), we have received numerous accolades, praise, and inquiries from colleagues across the nation regarding our efforts that made such a tremendous impact. I believe *It Takes A Campus* can serve as a guide for campus professionals, who are in the early stages of their retention efforts, as well as for seasoned retention gurus, who are seeking to improve existing programs or identify specific initiatives that proved effective and adapt them to their own student population. Unlike several research intensive books by well-known higher education theorists, *It Takes A Campus* is not one of them. My intentional design for this book is to be very practitioner-friendly, so higher education professionals who work daily with retention efforts, can create, modify, or assess retention initiatives on their campuses.

We all share the same goal of student success. If we are successful in achieving this goal with individual students, our retention rates will take care of themselves. Good luck in your retention efforts.

The University of Mississippi

Memorandum
PROVOST AND VICE CHANCELLOR FOR ACADEMIC AFFAIRS
Lyceum 137
University, MS 38677
Phone: (662) 915-5974 Fax: (662) 915-5280

TO: Distribution List

FROM: Provost

DATE: March 24, 2008

SUBJECT: Retention Task Force

During this past year, the Chancellor, as well as faculty and departments in academic affairs and student life, has recommended the creation of a Retention Task Force. The Retention Task Force would focus our efforts as an institution on increasing student retention and persistence rates with the ultimate goal of improving student success. The intent of such a task force is to understand the demographic shifts and changes in preparedness of our students so that we can develop a plan to bring about meaningful changes on our campus. I would be grateful if you would serve on this task force.

Associate Provost and Vice Chancellor for Student Affairs have agreed to co-chair the Retention Task Force. Please let the Provost's secretary know as quickly as possible if you can serve at [extension] or [email]. I think this will be a tremendous opportunity to identify ways that we can help the University and our students.

Thank you very much.

Distribution List:

School of Business Associate Dean/Faculty
Career Center Director
Assistant Vice Chancellor for Student Affairs
Sociology Department Chair/Faculty
Mathematics Department Chair/Faculty
Academic Support Center Assistant Director
Registrar
Music Department Chair/Faculty
School of Business Assistant to the Dean
Financial Aid Associate Director
Nutrition and Hospitality Management
    Department Faculty
Student Housing Director
School of Education Assistant Dean/Faculty

Center for Excellence in Teaching and
    Learning Assistant Director
Office of Outreach and Continuing Education
    Director of Credit Programs
School of Engineering Faculty
Student Disability Services Director
College of Liberal Arts Assistant Dean/Faculty
School of Accountancy Faculty
Counseling Center Director
Admissions Director
Institutional Research Data Analyst
Assistant Dean of Students
School of Pharmacy Faculty
Associate Provost
Vice Chancellor for Student Affairs

INITIATIVE 1
SUPPORT FROM THE TOP

CREATING A RETENTION TASK FORCE

On March 24, 2008, I was asked to be a part of the newly created Retention Task Force. When this task force was created, the University's yearly First Time Full Time (FTFT) retention hovered in the upper 70% range. The chancellor and provost wanted a wide array of campus professionals to take a critical look at retention and how the University could better serve our students. The initial task force had 26 members from across campus and was chaired by the vice chancellor for student affairs and the associate provost. Membership of the task force included representatives from a number of departments (see following table).

The provost at the inaugural meeting stressed the importance of improving the University's freshman retention rate. He stressed that improving our retention rate was one of his and the chancellor's major priorities for the foreseeable future. Following the provost's charge, Institutional Research presented data regarding our prior retention rates and how we compared to other Southern University Group (SUG) institutions. The remaining time was spent discussing our initial thoughts on

School/Department/Division	Title
School of Business	Associate Dean/Faculty
Career Center	Director
Student Affairs	Assistant Vice Chancellor
Sociology Department	Department Chair/Faculty
Mathematics Department	Department Chair/Faculty
Academic Support Center	Assistant Director
Registrar's Office	Registrar
Music Department	Department Chair/Faculty
School of Business	Assistant to the Dean
Financial Aid	Associate Director
Nutrition and Hospitality Management Department	Faculty
Student Housing	Director
School of Education	Assistant Dean/Faculty
Center for Excellence in Teaching and Learning	Assistant Director
Office of Outreach and Continuing Education	Director of Credit Programs
School of Engineering	Faculty
Student Disability Services	Director
College of Liberal Arts	Associate Dean/Faculty
School of Accountancy	Faculty
Counseling Center	Director
Admissions	Director
Institutional Research	Data Analyst
Dean of Students	Assistant Dean
School of Pharmacy	Faculty
*Provost Office	Associate Provost
*Student Affairs	Vice Chancellor
*Chairs of the Retention Task Force	

retention and dividing the group into subcommittees. The four subcommittees included: 1) Overview of Previous Efforts; 2) Inventory of Current Activities, Programs, and Services; 3) Best Practices; and 4) Data Development.

During this time period I was the assistant director for the Academic Support Center (ASC). The ASC provided academic advising to undeclared students and coordinated several academic support programs. My role on the committee was to represent academic advising and academic support initiatives for freshmen at the University. I was asked to serve on the Inventory of Current Activities, Programs, and Services Subcommittee. Over the course of the summer and fall semester, the subcommittees compiled information in their respected areas.

The Retention Task Force completed a final report and made six recommendations to the provost in the fall of 2008: 1) create a retention office; 2) restructure EDLD 105 as a three credit-hour, optional first-year experience course for all new freshmen; 3) require EDLD 101 in the spring term for all freshmen who were placed on academic probation at the end of the fall semester; 4) review and streamline first-year cohort programs and summer experiences for freshmen; 5) develop a supplemental instruction program for improving student success in large classes and courses with relatively low student success rates; 6) review and realign the University's Contractual Readmission Program to make it more comprehensive.

After presenting the retention report to the provost, discussions ensued rapidly about how to best implement the recommendations of the Retention Task Force. However, the University was dealing with an environment of budget constraints and a lack of resources to hire new staff to devote to the retention efforts. With no comprehensive funding in the immediate future, the Office of the Provost had to be creative in order to increase freshmen retention. It was clear that a comprehensive, campus-wide retention strategy among all stakeholders in our campus community needed to be implemented.

At this juncture, the first recommendation of a dedicated office of retention could not be established. The provost then asked key members of the Retention Task Force to form an eight-member committee to lead retention efforts. He asked the co-chairs of the initial group to lead the newly titled Retention Steering Committee and charged the committee to go forward with the implementation of the other recommended policies, activities, and initiatives directed to increase retention rates. Along with the co-chairs, group members included Financial Aid, Academic Support Center, Center for Excellence in Teaching and Learning, Faculty, College of Liberal Arts Dean's Office, Student Affairs, and Institutional Research and Assessment.

On November 5, 2008, the provost called an initial meeting of the Retention Steering Committee. There was a need to take some immediate steps toward intervention with the fall semester's current freshmen. Part of the impetus for these more immediate action steps was due to the committee learning that nearly 10% of the enrolled fall freshman class does not return for the spring semester. The committee also learned that the retention rate for the 2007 freshman cohort had declined to 78.3%, and the provost had asked the group to take action with the 2008 freshman cohort. Committee efforts were successful–81% of the 2008 freshman cohort returned for their second year.

Through the committee-approach over the past several years, the University has learned a great deal about factors that impact student retention while raising the University's freshman retention rate. The contact efforts and initiatives of the Retention Steering Committee involve many University offices. It has been especially gratifying to see the cooperation from numerous campus colleagues. Although the retention group has changed names and membership since 2008, we continue to explore all factors affecting freshman retention and are committed to helping our students be successful.

Provost Support for Retention Initiatives

With the Retention Steering Committee leading the University's retention efforts, the provost felt confident in supporting most of the group's initial recommendations. Some of the recommended initiatives from the original Retention Task Force that the provost supported included (a) a comprehensive first-year experience course; (b) a mandatory study skills course for freshman on academic probation; (c) a readmission program that would allow students to return to the University without sitting out a semester after being placed on academic suspension; (d) a supplemental instruction program. Additionally, the provost agreed to fund, provide space, and offer support for an academic advising model that provided professional advisors for the majority of freshmen. I will provide more details about these initiatives throughout the book.

The revitalization of our first-year experience (FYE) course, EDHE 105, on our campus has been very beneficial in our retention efforts. Fortunately, the provost understood the benefits of a robust FYE course. Supporting our need to make the course worth three credit hours and letter-graded was extremely helpful. Additionally, his financial support in allowing us to staff the course ensured we had a sustainable model for course instructors.

Similar to EDHE 105, the provost also supported the committee's recommendation to make EDHE 101 "Academic Skills for College," a required course for all new freshmen who were placed on academic probation following their first semester at the University. Prior to this requirement, EDHE 101 was optional for freshmen on academic probation. Several years of data indicated that students who chose to enroll in the course earned a higher semester GPA, and were retained at higher levels than their peers who had the option to take the course, but chose not to enroll. We also received approval for a funding model in which we could pay EDHE 101 instructors. Prior to this funding approval, the course was primarily taught by volunteers or graduate assistants. The funding was provided from a course fee, which also was approved during the policy change to make this a required course.

The Contractual Readmission Program (CRP) was a new initiative, which other peer institutions had found to be successful. This academic support program allowed students on academic suspension to return to the University without sitting out a semester. Prior to this option being supported by the provost, students who went from academic probation to academic suspension were required to sit out the following semester unless they made a 2.0 GPA in 12 credit hours of summer school coursework at the University or successfully appealed for the right to return. While students were sitting out, they were not allowed to take courses at another institution and have the credits transfer back to the University of Mississippi. Unfortunately, many of the students who went on academic suspension and left the University never returned. The CRP was an excellent option for students who fell short academically, but who understood how they could improve with the proper academic guidance. Students who wanted to pursue the CRP option signed an agreement that spelled out the program's requirements and interviewed with an academic consultant. Academic support was provided to CRP students throughout the semester.

The final recommendation from the Retention Task Force was to create an effective Supplemental Instruction (SI) program. SI consisted of weekly review sessions that reinforced course content. The sessions were led by upperclassmen who previously did well in the course. Some of the first classes chosen to participate in SI were Accountancy 201, Biology 160, and Chemistry 105. These courses were known to be some of the most academically challenging gateway courses on our campus. The SI program was coordinated within the Center for Excellence in Teaching and Learning.

An initiative that was not recommended by the Retention Task Force, but one that the provost has supported over the years, was to move away from a primarily faculty-only academic advising model and transitioning to professional staff advisors when working with new freshmen. The philosophy behind this model was to provide total support (e.g., academic and non-academic) to new freshmen at the University. Professional staff academic advisors could address all issues related to being successful during the first year. The provost in 2011 proposed to the deans the idea of utilizing professional advisors for freshmen. One school, the School of Applied Sciences, volunteered to allow their freshmen to be advised by professional advisors in the Academic Support Center. Applied Sciences was very pleased with the outcome, as their faculty advising load was reduced, faculty could spend more time with upperclassmen and graduate students more committed to their majors, and the School's first-year retention rate increased by almost 5%. Other schools took notice and wanted to offer the same type of support to their first-year freshmen. However, this would require a tremendous amount of resources and a shift in the way the University had previously supported new freshmen.

Provost Support for New Center

After the new initiatives had time to be established, assessed, and revised, data indicated that our efforts were working as more first-year students were being retained than ever before. Unfortunately, our model of various programs and initiatives spread throughout campus made coordination difficult. The provost and vice chancellor of student affairs viewed this as an opportunity to create an all-inclusive center that would support "anything and everything freshman."

The newly created Center would be known as the Center for Student Success and First-Year Experience (CSSFYE). Initially, the Center housed four student support units: Academic Advising, First-Year Experience, Veteran and Military Services, and Freshman Retention. Two years later Academic Support Programs was moved from the Center for Excellence in Teaching and Learning to the CSSFYE. Each unit within the Center plays a vital role in student success.

Committee efforts were successful—81% of the 2008 freshman cohort returned for their second year.

The University of Mississippi recognizes that quality academic advising can have a significant impact on student success. Professional academic advisors have the ability to address "anything and everything freshman." This includes most academic and non-academic issues. CSSFYE advisors begin interacting with new freshmen at Summer Orientation and continue their communication with new freshmen throughout the summer and their first academic year. Our Center currently employs nine full-time professionals who advise students.

When the Retention Steering Committee recommended a three credit-hour, letter-graded First-Year Experience (FYE) course, we never imagined it would become a best practice initiative and receive recognition throughout higher education. During the early iterations of the course, the Associate Director of Financial Aid coordinated and assessed

> The University of Mississippi recognizes that quality academic advising can have a significant impact on student success.

all aspects. However, this model was not sustainable, as the number of sections increased dramatically each year. The class is currently taught every semester and summer sessions, with 126 sections offered each fall. Creating an FYE Unit that is responsible for EDHE 105, other courses, and additional initiatives has truly been a benefit for everyone.

Veteran and Military Services was a new unit that needed a home. A single program coordinator initially staffed this office. However, once the unit was moved under the CSSFYE additional employees, including a Veterans Administration (VA) Certifying Official and several VA student workers were hired. The progress this unit has made in supporting our student-veterans has been tremendous. Student-veterans can now get most of their issues addressed in one convenient location. Additionally, the increased programming for student-veterans, training for faculty and staff, and other means of support has been well received by this special population.

As previously mentioned, freshman retention has received much attention over the last few years. Including a freshman retention unit within the CSSFYE was a wise decision. Although only one person has the word "retention" in her title—assistant director-retention—it is an all-hands-on-deck approach in the CSSFYE. The assistant director-retention serves on the University's Retention Advisory Board, creates, analyzes, and distributes numerous reports, and coordinates retention efforts that are carried out by the CSSFYE Staff. Later in this book I will discuss the importance of having a point person for retention.

Academic Support Programs (ASP) is the newest unit within the CSSFYE. Although some of the programs and classes housed within this unit do not directly impact first-year students, there are four specific initiatives that do contribute to first-year students being successful and retained. EDHE 101 "Academic Skills for College" is a mandatory three credit-hour, letter graded course for new freshmen who are placed on academic probation after their first semester. The Contractual Readmission Program (CRP) is a total support program that allows students who are placed on academic suspension to remain at the University. These students must apply, and be accepted, to the program. The CRP utilizes a mandatory academic support course, weekly meetings with a peer mentor or professional staff member, and required guidance from other offices on campus (e.g., Advising, Financial Aid, etc.). Another program that has been successful is Academic Consultations. Students can volunteer to meet with a graduate peer mentor or professional staff member on a weekly basis. Meetings can ensure the student stays on track with time management, class assignments, and other pertinent components of being success-

Creating an FYE Unit that is responsible for EDHE 105, other courses, and additional initiatives has truly been a benefit for everyone.

ful at the University. Finally, the Do It Yourself (DIY) Workshops are great for individuals or groups of students who are looking for specific strategies to improve the study skills. Some common DIY Workshops include: Time Management, Test Preparation, and College Note Taking. Since the Center's opening, the provost has stated numerous times that one of his greatest accomplishments was the creation of the CSSFYE.

Provost Support for Collaborative Efforts

Even though the Center for Student Success and First-Year Experience resides in the Division of Student Affairs, we rely heavily on collaborating with departments all across campus. From academic affairs, administration and finance, to other student affairs departments, we value partnerships that foster student success on our campus. I have heard numerous colleagues at other institutions discuss departments on their campuses that operate in silos. Although we are not perfect, when it comes to student success and persistence of our first-year freshmen, silos are not an issue at the University of Mississippi.

When thinking about collaborating with academic affairs, several programs and initiatives immediately come to mind. Our professional academic advisors work closely with the deans' offices whose freshmen we advise. We can keep them abreast of current student measurements (e.g., persistence, academic standing, etc.) and they meet regularly with us to inform on policy, curriculum, and other changes that are directly related to their school/college. Additionally, several of our partnering schools/college utilize freshmen faculty mentors. Our academic advisors remind students of their faculty mentors and how to contact them. Data sharing with academic affairs is also very important. Our assistant director-retention shares data with campus professionals who have been designated as special cohort owners. For

> We value partnerships that foster student success on our campus.

example, we will send the owners of FASTrack, Provost Scholars, Honors College, and others detailed lists of their freshmen who have yet to register. The list will include pertinent information such as student I.D., name, phone numbers, and e-mail addresses. These owners will contact their "no schedule" freshmen and share notes with our Center. Partnering with academic affairs in our retention efforts has been beneficial.

One of the more underrated collaborations on our campus is the interaction with the Division of Administration and Finance. Each semester after priority registration has ended, we send the provost a list of all freshmen who have yet to register. The provost reviews the list and finds a cut-off point for balances owed by those freshmen. The provost then asks the Bursar to temporarily remove their Bursar Hold. The cut-off amount is usually between $200-$400 and the hold removal lasts approximately two weeks. By temporarily removing this hold, the student can register for courses in a timely manner. We see a significant number of freshmen who owe a small balance register during this short time period. Having a good relationship with the Bursar's Office allows a cooperative effort to help with freshmen who owe money (outside the small balance owed during the previously mentioned two-week window) on a case-by-case basis. The debts are still owed by the student, but under certain circumstances the Bursar will temporarily remove the Bursar Hold for a 24-hour period if a student is working with one of our academic advisors. Financial concerns continue to be our leading cause for lack of persistence. Any assistance we can receive in addressing this issue is greatly appreciated, and the Bursar is definitely an ally you want on your side.

Under the leadership of our provost and the vice chancellor for student affairs, it has become widely known that the University places great emphasis on our retention efforts. Their public support allows us to easily collaborate with other departments within the Division of Student Affairs. Some of the most common reasons for a freshman's departure are issues that fall under Student Affairs. Of the top five reasons students cite for leaving the University, four of them could be addressed with Student Affairs: financial concerns, social fit, homesickness/distance from home, and health issues. There are too many examples to name here, but one could easily point out other important collaborations, including the Career Center, Counseling Center, Financial Aid, Student Housing, Student Conduct, Campus Recreation, Student Health, Admissions/Orientation, and Dean of Students. Because financial issues are our primary reason for a freshman's lack of persistence, we are very appreciative of the Office of Financial Aid's efforts. Two members from Financial Aid (director and associate director) serve on our Retention Advisory Board and are committed to doing all they can to assist us as it relates to financial barriers. One cannot say enough about their work with individual freshmen who are having financial concerns. Student retention is truly a team effort in Student Affairs.

Under the leadership of our provost and the vice chancellor for student affairs, it has become widely known that the University places great emphasis on our retention efforts.

Support from the Top

Identify your current levels of support from top administrators.
Who (President, Provost, Vice-Presidents, Deans, etc.):

_____

_____

_____

_____

_____

Types of support (financial, human resources, space, promoting your efforts, etc.):

_____

_____

_____

_____

_____

Brainstorm ways to increase support from top administrators.

_____

_____

_____

_____

_____

_____

_____

Interview

Dr. Ann Canty

Former Associate Provost and co-chair of the
inaugural Retention Task Force

Describe your former role in the University of Mississippi's retention efforts.

Retention at the University of Mississippi was a topic of concern for many years. In fact, numerous programmatic activities aimed at the freshman student were in place during the 1990s, and various departments and academic units developed their own programs to increase both enrollment and retention. We had many retention activities in the School of Business Administration when I was Associate Dean for Undergraduate Programs, but only for the Business students and not for students across the campus. It's been said that "retention is everybody's business," and that's true, but no department or unit at the University was responsible for evaluation of retention data or evaluation of the programs that were created to retain the Ole Miss Freshman student.

Recognizing the importance of a campus-wide retention effort, the chancellor and provost proposed the creation of a Retention Task Force composed of faculty and staff from academic affairs and student affairs in the spring of 2008. It was agreed that it was important for both academics and student affairs to work together and to collaborate on student retention. The Task Force was charged with developing a focus on the University's efforts to increase student retention and persistence rates with the ultimate goal of improving student success. By this time, I held the position of Associate Provost, and served as a co-chair of the 26-member Retention Task Force, along with the vice chancellor for student affairs. The Task Force was divided into four subcommittees with appointed leaders to investigate areas with an impact on retention:

1. Overview of previous efforts at the University of Mississippi
2. Inventory of current programs, activities, and services
3. Best practices that have been implemented at other universities
4. Data development

After reports from the subcommittees and helpful input from the Deans' Offices and Financial Aid, the Task Force members knew there was a need for ongoing planning and consistency in retention activities. With information from the subcommittees, we learned that first-year student success is a critical aspect of success at the University of Mississippi, but no single program or activity had a significant impact on retention. To continue the retention initiative, a Retention Steering Committee was established composed of ten members from critical areas of the University such as Financial Aid, the Academic Support Center, Institutional Research, College of Liberal Arts, Student Affairs, and faculty. The vice chancellor for student affairs and I continued our co-chair roles.

In fall, 2008, the new Retention Steering Committee learned that the retention rate for the 2007 cohort had declined to 78.3%, and the provost asked the Committee to take immediate action steps. There was a consensus to use all means available to us to connect with freshmen students and encourage them to pre-assign for spring 2009. We had research that indicated students who pre-assigned for the following semester were more inclined to return. Activities included sample letters for deans to send to their students, advisor contacts, Facebook ads, updated spreadsheets for deans to show the students who had not pre-assigned, Financial Aid contact for students with financial needs, personal contact in the residence halls, and continuing email and personal phone calls to students proved successful. The Retention Steering Committee had succeeded in the short term and began to plan for consistency in their activities going forward.

In your opinion, what are some of the most effective retention strategies we implemented at the University?

Everyone involved in the task force and steering committee believed that any retention initiative should be one that helped students make a successful transition from a high school environment to the university setting. The important aspect of that transition was a student knowing his or her University advisor. The Academic Support Center advised all of the undecided majors in 2008. Other schools and colleges advised their majors. We learned that students who were advised in Orientation in June and July were often unsure about contacting their advisor when pre-assignment rolled around in November and even in April in spring semester. The Academic Support Center began advising more of the freshmen students from all schools and colleges. Students knew their advisors and returned to the same advisor in the same office when pre-assignment time came. Advisors were added and the Academic Support Center became the Center for Student Success and First-Year Experience.

The University had an elective course, EDHE 105, with limited sections that involved study skills for the freshman students. Reworking the curriculum and increasing the sections of this course with creative funding, provided a seat for each freshman student and has evolved into a First-Year Experience Course with 120 sections. EDHE 101, a study skills course, was streamlined for freshmen to take in the spring semester if they were on probation.

Data from Institutional Research provided up to date information for personal letters and phone calls to freshmen from dedicated staff members. These data were invaluable in contacting students about financial aid, scholarships, mid-term grades, and reports to advisors.

Supplemental Instruction (SI) is a program of academic support that is designed for courses with large lecture classes with relatively low student success rates. SI sessions were created by the Center for Teaching and Learning, providing students with opportunities for deeper engagement with class material. The sessions are led by trained facilitators who have had the course and have been successful.

Since you became involved in the University's retention efforts, describe some changes you observed.

With the ultimate goal of student success, there have been many changes at the University. There is a new Center for Student Success and First Year Experience. The retention rate increased for the 2007 cohort from 78.3% to 86.5% in 2015. The Steering Committee learned that there is a 90% historical correlation between retention rates and graduation rates at the University of Mississippi. With the increase in retention rates, we have also seen an increase in graduation rates. The Bachelor of General Studies, which is a degree program that focuses on bringing previous students back to campus, is a great change. Enrollment of the freshman class has continued to rise. The increased enrollment is not surprising since word-of-mouth on student services and especially freshmen assistance is significant for parents and students.

Where do you see retention efforts going in the short term? Long term?

I anticipate the retention efforts continuing, and additional staff and faculty added to respond to the freshmen needs in the long term. We know that advising is strength of the University and can make a difference in retention. Since enrollment has continued to grow at the University, the enrollment growth in the short term may impact the retention rate negatively. However, I anticipate the stabilization in human resources and services to freshman students will also stabilize the retention rate and increase the graduation rate. Data gathering directed to these efforts will continue.

What advice would you give other institutions regarding their retention efforts?

My advice to other institutions is to start at the top. With leadership from the Provost Office and involvement of deans and administrators, a group can be formed that works on retention fervently. At the time of our efforts, the University was dealing with an environment of budget constraints and a lack of resources to hire new staff to devote to the retention. With a data driven effort and involvement of faculty and staff across the University, the Retention Steering Committee became an instrument of change. Advisors were involved at every point and creative ideas were accepted by administrators and acted upon by advisors and leaders of freshman activities.

INITIATIVE 2
HAVING A POINT PERSON

Anyone who has ever worked in student retention has heard the phrase: "Retention is everyone's responsibility." Unfortunately, when something is "everyone's responsibility" it can also be considered no one's responsibility. For many years the University of Mississippi had a "retention is everyone's responsibility" attitude. That philosophy lead to upper-70% range retention rates. However, when the University's leadership made the decision to make retention a primary responsibility for several University staff and faculty members, the freshman retention rates rose to the mid-80% range. The increased rates from the structural change supported the notion that when someone or a small group of dedicated professionals takes ownership, the results will outperform a model where everyone has a responsibility, but no specific person is held accountable.

When the University's leadership made the decision to make retention a primary responsibility for several University staff and faculty members, the freshman retention rates rose to the mid-80% range.

Retention Steering Committee Leadership

The first people to be accountable for freshman retention at the University of Mississippi were the co-chairs of the inaugural Retention Steering Committee in 2008. These initial faces of freshman retention belonged to the associate provost and the vice chancellor for student affairs. During the early years of the Retention Steering Committee the co-chairs dictated the work of the committee, gathered data, backed new retention-related programs, and reported committee ideas and concerns directly to the provost. Additionally, with these two professionals being in key leadership positions, they had the power and respect to get things accomplished. The first few years of their leadership laid the groundwork for many of the programs, policies, and support that we continue to rely on to this day. Although the leadership and, later, the name of the Retention Steering Committee have changed, their accountability for freshman retention has remained constant. In fact, some could argue there is more accountability than ever before due to the increased resources (e.g., funding, staff, space, support, etc.) dedicated to freshman retention.

Presently, the Retention Advisory Board is co-chaired by the director of the Center for Student Success and First-Year Experience (me) and the assistant dean for the College of Liberal Arts. This partnership has been very beneficial as the two leaders represent both student affairs and academic affairs. As co-chair, I feel personally responsible for increasing the University's freshman retention rate. Initiatives that I feel would be successful can be vetted through the Retention Advisory Board, then passed up to the provost and vice chancellor for student affairs. Both leaders have been very supportive and trust that everything I suggest is in the best interest of student satisfaction, success, and persistence.

I have found that having a co-chair from academic affairs is a key component to our success. My co-chair is able to get the support from fellow faculty members and deans' offices. Even though academic issues are not significant motives for freshmen leaving the University, gaining support from the academic side of the house is paramount. From my experience, deans' offices and faculty members want our freshmen to be successful and persist, but do not know how to help. This is especially true when they review our retention data and see that most freshmen cite non-academic issues as the primary reason for the lack of persistence. By having a fellow academic scholar advising them on what is in the best interest of retention has increased buy-in. For example, more faculty are becoming aware and supporting our desire to create specialized cohorts within the freshman cohort. Additionally, by publicizing the success rates and effectiveness of our First-Year Experience course (EDHE 105), an increased number of academic departments are volunteering to have special sections dedicated to their freshman majors. These departments even offer their own staff members to teach specialized sections. Having an administrator in academic affairs as co-chair of the Retention Advisory Board is a win-win situation for both the University and the students. I am hopeful the University will always support the work of the Retention Advisory Board, and hold the leaders of this group accountable for freshman retention. The results from this model continue to move the freshman retention needle in the right direction.

An Office Accountable for Retention

I am aware that some institutions have an office or center with the word "Retention" in the title and the primary purpose of the unit is to increase retention. The University of Mississippi does not have a specific office dedicated to retention, but does have a center in which freshman retention is part of the mission. At the Center for Student Success and First-Year Experience (CSSFYE) our five units have student success and persistence interwoven into everything we do. The Center has five leaders who oversee the individual units and report to the director.

Center Leaders

Associate Director: Oversight of all first-year experience initiatives including EDHE 105 "Freshman Year Experience" for new freshmen (130 sections in Fall 2015), EDHE 305 "Transfer Student Experience (18 sections in Fall 2015), Partnership for Student Success–a partnership program with a local community college for non-residents who were not admitted to the University for the fall, but live on campus while taking classes at the community college, serves on the University's Retention Advisory Board, co-chairs the University's Transfer Student Task Force, and other responsibilities.

Assistant Director-Advising: Our Assistant Director-Advising supervises nine professional academic advisors, who support approximately 75% of the freshman cohort, oversees the Academic Advising Network, coordinates various meet and greets for new freshmen, and other student success initiatives. With our academic advisors addressing "anything and everything freshman," teaching EDHE 105, and various other contributions to our student success efforts, this frontline unit has been vital in our retention efforts.

Assistant Director-Retention: This position has been crucial to our retention efforts. From coordinating the First-Year Attendance Based Initiative to creating and disseminating data reports all across campus, no one person has played a more pivotal role in our retention success than our assistant director-retention. Additionally, this person serves on the University's Retention Advisory Board, is the lead data professional for the Non-Resident Admissions Committee, and coordinates almost all inter-Center retention efforts.

Assistant Director-Academic Support Programs: The newest unit within the Center is our Academic Support Programs. This Assistant Director is responsible for coordinating EDHE 101 "Academic Skills for College" for freshmen who are placed on academic probation after their first semester (36 sections in Spring 2016), EDHE 202 "Fundamentals of Active Learning" for students returning from academic suspension or dismissal, our new EDHE 303 "Academic Skills for Transfer Students" (first sections in Spring 2016), academic consultations, and other important student success initiatives.

Coordinator of Veteran and Military Services: Military veterans, active service men and women, and dependents are a very important special population at the University. For many years this group was served through a variety of offices. Unfortunately, these decentralized efforts were not conducive to this population feeling like the University had their best interests in mind. Although we still have room for improvement, over the last three years since the unit's creation, veterans and military members are more efficiently served at the University. By having a centralized support unit, new veterans and military students are identified upon their admission to the University. From the moment they step foot on campus at orientation, to the paperwork they must complete each semester, this unit actively engages and supports our veteran and military students to the best of their ability.

Even though each unit within the Center has its own primary responsibilities, student success, satisfaction, and persistence are paramount in each of our daily activities. During weekly staff meetings we discuss everything related to the CSSFYE. This includes how student success and retention is related to day-to-day job functions, upcoming programs and events, courses taught under our supervision, and other facets in which the Center has oversight. Furthermore, CSSFYE leaders meet every other week. This meeting allows all Center leaders to be informed on each person's area of oversight. During these small group meetings, collaboration may occur among the units. For example, the Assistant Director-Retention may need the academic advisors to contact all freshmen who have two or more D's or F's at mid-term. The assistant director-retention will create a report to share with the assistant director-advising. The report also will be shared with the academic advisors. The assistant director-advising will then follow up with the academic advisors. The Associate Director also can ask the assistant director-retention to create a similar report for all freshmen enrolled in EDHE 105 who have two or more D's or F's at mid-term. The associate director will share the report with all EDHE 105 instructors and follow up as needed. Having several student success units under one center has been valuable in our retention efforts.

Resources

In 2010 the University's Academic Support Center had six employees, one central office, and a much smaller budget. As the support for professional advisors working with freshmen became a priority, we hired four new advisors and acquired additional space. Once the new Center for Student Success and First-Year Experience was created, and the aforementioned units were to be housed here, we gained additional personnel, space, and larger operating budgets. We now have a staff of 35 campus professionals (18 professional staff and 17 graduate assistants), increased financial support, larger space that is spread throughout two buildings, and top level support for our initiatives. These increased resources have been vital to our success. In a world where units are told to do more with less, we have been fortunate. When asked to support more students, programs, and classes, we have been given the resources needed to ensure the increased responsibilities would be effective.

Question:

How can having multiple units under one center be beneficial?

One does not have to dig deep to see our increased support already paying dividends. For several years our EDHE 105 course was taught by campus professionals on a volunteer basis. Most of these professionals were under student affairs. Department directors who allowed their staff to teach were compensated with a $500 honorarium. This model worked well for approximately 50 sections of the course. The combination of a growing freshman class and the popularity of the course, made it apparent we needed to consider a new compensation model in order to attract more instructors. The CSSFYE submitted a proposal to the vice chancellor of student affairs and the provost to pay instructors a $2,000 stipend. Fortunately, the proposal was approved and staffing has not been an issue as we now offer 130 sections of EDHE 105 each fall semester. Instructors can choose the $500 honorarium for their department or take 35 hours' vacation leave and be paid the $2,000 stipend. Of the 130 sections in the

Fall 2015 semester, approximately 65% of instructors chose the $2,000 stipend. This equated to $243,880 in salaries and fringe benefits to instructors of EDHE 105. The increased financial support for EDHE 105 instructors not only made it easier to recruit enough, but allowed us to increase the quality. We now have an instructor waitlist and review process for new instructors wanting to teach the course. The stipend model worked so well, that we have also adapted it to our EDHE 101 course.

Space on our campus is always in high demand. The provost once said he could fund a new position much easier than he could provide space for the employee. That is why I have been very appreciative when we received new space during our significant growth period. In 2015 when the Center took over Academic Support Programs (ASP) from the Center for Excellence in Teaching and Learning, my primary concern was space for new staff and their programs. Currently, the ASP staff members and graduate assistants are located in another building on campus. The distance between the two buildings makes supervision and collaboration less than ideal. Fortunately, we have been allocated a large space in a building that is under renovation. This building is very close to our other offices, and I and the assistant director-academic support programs have been involved in the renovation plans. Meetings with Facilities Planning, architects, and engineers have allowed us to design our ideal space for staff and programs. The new space will not be ready until 2017, but we are very excited and grateful for this phenomenal student support opportunity.

Student Data

During the 2015-16 academic year the Center for Student Success and First Year Experience worked with thousands of University of Mississippi students. Many of these students were members of our freshman cohort. I am confident our professional staff, programs, courses, and support played a role in helping our students be satisfied, successful, and retained at the University.

Academic Advising

Students Helped	9200
Students Advised	5902
Academic Advising Network Attendees	388
Total	15490

First-Year Experience

EDHE 105 sections for fall/spring/summer	134
EDHE 305 sections for fall/spring	26
EDHE 310/311 sections for fall/spring	2
EDHE 105 enrolled for fall/spring/summer	2911
EDHE 305 enrolled for fall/spring	485
EDHE 310/311 enrolled for fall/spring	59
Attendees at presentations	2427
Ole Miss Opportunity Participants	322
Partnership for Student Success Participants	52
One-on-One Counseling	891
Presentations, Tours, etc.	80
Total	7147

Academic Support Programs

EDHE 101 sections for fall/spring	31
EDHE 202 sections for fall/spring	80
EDHE 303 sections for spring	3
EDHE 101 enrolled for fall/spring	426
EDHE 202 enrolled for fall/spring	835
EDHE 303 enrolled for spring	54
Contractual Readmission Program Participants	373
Do It Yourself (DIY) Attendees	60
Peer Leadership Attendees	59
Academic consultations	240
Total	2047

Veteran and Military Services

Veteran students assisted	1686
Military students assisted	841
Military dependent students assisted	1464
Parents (current/future) assisted	569
VA Certifications	2761
Faculty and staff development	122
SVA Meeting (Student-led)	113
Total	7556

Dr. Kyle Ellis moderating a panel at the University's At Risk Student Summit

THREE PEOPLE WHO THINK
ABOUT RETENTION DAILY

In my opinion, at least one person (if not multiple people) on a campus needs to lead an institution's retention efforts. When I hear the phrase "retention is everyone's responsibility," I immediately think, "When can we get everyone together to discuss retention, when can we get everyone's retention reports, and when does everyone have retention components factored into their evaluations?" I have come to realize that when everyone is in charge, then ultimately, no one is in charge.

At the University of Mississippi there are three people who think about retention on a daily basis. Other than me, as director of the CSS-FYE and co-chair of the University's Retention Advisory Board, our assistant director-retention and the assistant vice chancellor for student affairs are the other two people who think daily about retention. Having specific point people has several advantages. When the provost or vice chancellor for student affairs has retention-related questions, concerns, or data needs, they can contact any of us. Usually they contact me first, but it is not uncommon for me to confer with the other two before responding and providing information. By having a small consolidated group, we are much more expeditious in our fulfillment of their requests, as opposed to a model where everyone is in charge of retention.

Question:

Who thinks about retention daily on your campus?

Have specific people responsible for retention on your campus.

One of the greatest assets in our efforts is the high value that the assistant director-retention and I place on retention in all of our daily job responsibilities. Our offices are located next to each other. It is not uncommon for other staff members to walk into the middle of a retention-related conversation occurring between our offices. There have been numerous days where almost every conversation revolved around retention. We both place such a high priority on retention and know the other person can relate to whatever is occurring. Some of our colleagues find it funny that when any news breaks that could factor into our retention, our first question is "Was it a freshman?" If a student athlete gets dismissed from a team, a student gets arrested, or other potential departure news, we have become so ingrained in retention efforts, that it is a natural reaction to hope the student was not in the freshman cohort.

Other than developing a shared way of thinking in regard to retention, the collaboration shared between me and our assistant director-retention is amazing. We work well together in that she provides me with a lot of retention data, which I use to interact with colleagues across campus. Furthermore, we are constantly bouncing ideas off another. As we see deficits in the retention data,

Leslie Banahan, Jennifer Phillips, and Kyle Ellis are three people who think about retention daily at the University of Mississippi.

we brainstorm possible initiatives to address the gaps. This year's regional/state meet and greets for freshmen became a reality after our conversation about the number of freshmen who left the University last year citing distance from home as the primary factor. It is difficult to put into words how valuable our partnership is as it relates to our retention efforts. When people from other institutions ask me to pick the primary component of a successful retention program, my response is almost always to have specific people responsible for retention on their campuses. Furthermore, being the only retention figurehead on campus can be stressful and cause burnout. Therefore, I highly recommend having more than one person to share the highs and lows, but more importantly, to help each other keep a positive outlook, as well as their sanity.

Having a Point Person

Identify your key people in retention efforts.
> Who (upper level down to front line professionals):

_____

_____

_____

_____

> Primary functions of these people (total oversight, policy makers, ability to create and implement initiatives, front line work with the initiatives, etc.):

_____

_____

_____

_____

Brainstorm ways to identify a specific point person if one is not currently in existence. If a point person is already identified, lists ways this person can increase his/her role in retention efforts.

_____

_____

_____

_____

_____

INTERVIEW

Jennifer Phillips
CSSFYE Assistant Director-Retention

Describe your role in the University's retention efforts.

I am the Assistant Director for Retention. I am the hub of all the information that is collected regarding the freshman cohort. I organize the retention efforts in the Center for Student Success and coordinate those efforts across student affairs departments, academic departments, and holds owners. In addition to organizing the retention efforts, I run the data that are used for student contact, lists to departments and holds owners, and in-house lists.

In your opinion, what are some of the most effective retention strategies at the University?

I think the most effective retention strategy we have is the ability to know, as often as we would like, who is enrolled and who is not. Because of this, we are able to contact students within 24 hours or less of their academic departure at Ole Miss and do one of two things: 1) get a reason for departure (exit counseling); or, 2) assist the student in returning by helping them with whatever barrier they cite. Many times students are too quick to drop a schedule and not think about how they might be able to overcome the barrier that is presented to them. This personal touch is the most effective strategy that we have as an institution.

Another effective strategy is having a person who is the information hub. While retention is everyone's job, if no one is personally responsible for it then there is no ownership. I feel as though these are my students. I take it personally when they leave, especially when it could be helped. I see every student that is saved as a personal victory. I'm not sure you can have effective retention efforts without making a person or an office personally responsible.

Since you became involved in the University's retention efforts, describe some changes you have observed.

Several years ago, before the inception of the Center for Student Success and First-Year Experience, retention was an informal spreadsheet that was sent around the then Academic Support Center. This spreadsheet, that I maintained, was shared with Housing, Financial Aid, holds owners, and other groups. The information was not instantaneous. Now, we have implemented a retention tool that constituents across campus have access to in real time. Even though I keep my spreadsheet, I am no longer sending it around. People are able to look at the information they want anytime they would like and update information in the tool for others to see it. Not only can they update the tool, but they can choose individuals to whom they sent an alert that a note has been inputted.

Additionally, the creation of the Assistant Director for Retention position has helped create a centralized location for retention. Prior to that, no one was personally responsible for the retention data. Now that we are centralized, we know where every student went and why they left. That is a feat when tracking nearly 4,000 freshmen.

Also, instead of relying on Institutional Research (IR) to run reports, we have centralized reporting within our office. Rather than get a list of students who drop their schedules once a week from IR, we run it once a day in house. Additionally, depending on the time of year, we can run it as often as we like without bogging down IR's schedule.

The creation of the Retention Advisory Board was a huge step in retention initiatives. This Board has people from all across campus: student affairs offices, academic departments, and holds owners (especially financial). We meet once a month to discuss retention initiatives and brainstorm for ways we can help our students persist and graduate. Having all of these different constituents in the same room helps put things into perspective.

Where do you see retention efforts going in the short term? Long term?

I feel we will continue moving forward in our efforts both in the short and long terms. We have a dynamic team that is always looking forward to see what the next step will be with regard to retention initiatives. We are consistently refining what we are doing by deciding if it is working or not. If it isn't working, we decide whether to remove it completely or change it.

In the short term, I believe we will continue to tweak various programs as we get feedback from students. I also think we will become more data driven through new student surveys to target students before they have left.

In the long term, I believe we will try to connect even more users across campus through various technology initiatives. We will continue to educate people on warning signs to look for in students and how they can get students connected to people on campus who can help them.

What advice would you give other institutions regarding their retention efforts?

I would tell people two things: 1) you must have buy-in; and, 2) someone on campus needs to be passionately and personally responsible for retention. With regard to buy-in – you need support from various constituents on campus: Housing, Dean of Students, Academic Affairs, Student Affairs, Financial Aid, Bursar, etc. Try to think of anyone who can influence the reasons your students are leaving and create an advisory board to brainstorm the ways you can move your retention needle.

With regard to having someone passionately and personally responsible for retention – you must have a hub for information gathering. Pieces and parts of the same data set cannot be housed in different places on campus. This person needs to be passionate about helping students and simultaneously helping the institution. Some one person or department (ideally one person) needs to feel responsible for these students as if they all belong to him/her.

INITIATIVE 3
RETENTION ADVISORY BOARD

Although the Retention Advisory Board (formerly the Retention Task Force and Retention Steering Committee) has been mentioned throughout the first two initiatives, I feel this very important retention component deserves its own section within the book. The justification for creating the task force/committee/advisory board along with the group's history can be found in Initiative 1. My goal with this initiative is to discuss the important work the Retention Advisory Board currently oversees.

The Retention Advisory Board (RAB) is made up of 18 members from all across campus. The Board is co-chaired by the director of the Center for Student Success and First-Year Experience (me) and the assistant dean for the College of Liberal Arts. Each person on the Board brings a unique perspective and has oversight of at least one area that can influence freshman persistence. Even though members come from different areas of campus, we all share the same over-arching goal of helping

Having key members from across campus who share the same commitment to students is key in successful retention efforts.

our freshman cohort members be successful, satisfied, and persist at the University of Mississippi.

Before I discuss Board initiatives, responsibilities, and opportunities, I believe it would be valuable for me to list why specific members were chosen to the Board. Having key members from across campus who share the same commitment to students is key in successful retention efforts. If institutions are considering creating a group to oversee freshman retention, or looking to revise their current group's membership, I'm hopeful my rationale will be meaningful.

Assistant Vice Chancellor for Student Affairs: Many of our departments (Housing, Financial Aid, Student Success, etc.) that can have a direct impact on retention fall under the Division of Student Affairs. Having an administrator who can assist us in working with these departments on retention initiatives has proven to be helpful. Additionally, this person can gauge the vice chancellor for student affairs on potential Board items to see if there is initial interest and support. The valuable insight this person provides is a Board asset.

Financial Aid (Director and Associate Director): I cannot overstate how important it is to have Financial Aid representation on our Board. One of the most frequent responses given by students who leave the University is they are having "financial difficulties." Representatives' expertise and ability to offer suggestions on how to monetarily help students assist us in moving the retention needle is valuable. Furthermore, by establishing a good relationship with Financial Aid, they are willing to help individual students who are directly referred to them by key players in our retention efforts.

Information Technology: Our Information Technology (IT) representative is one of the new positions on the Board. This representative became a permanent fixture to the Board three years ago after the group consid-

We have found it difficult to keep faculty engaged in the Retention Advisor Board. Be sure to select faculty who are interested in student persistence.

ered purchasing retention software from an outside vendor. IT wanted our input regarding the primary functions of the proposed software. After careful consideration, IT decided they could create an in-house product with similar features. They were able to deliver what is now widely used on campus, The UM Retention Tool. Very creative name, right? Furthermore, by having the IT representative at all of our meetings and on the listserv, this person can quickly and efficiently address any Retention Tool or other IT-related issues, provide expert information from an IT perspective when discussing a new initiative, and inform us on best practices in the world of IT that are related to student retention.

Housing: Numerous colleagues from various colleges and universities have confirmed that campus professionals in their Student Housing Departments play a significant role in their student success and retention efforts. The University of Mississippi is no different in that we rely heavily on our partners in Student Housing. Although there is only

Student employees in housing participate in training prior to new freshmen moving in.

one official Student Housing representative on our Board, there are at least four different individuals I interact with in Student Housing as it relates to freshman retention. All of our freshman cohort members are required to live on campus, so having a professional from Student Housing is very helpful. This person updates us on new programs, offers input when we want to include Student Housing in a new initiative, and makes sure that traditional Student Housing retention-related tasks (e.g., Freshman Attendance Based Initiative follow ups, no schedule tracking, individual consultations and support to residents, and several others) are accomplished at the appropriate iterations.

Education-faculty/dean's office: It is very important to have faculty representation on a retention group. They can provide excellent insight from the academic side of the institution, and can garner support from other faculty members for various initiatives. However, from my experience it is difficult to find faculty who are willing to serve on a retention group. Over the past eight years, we have had various faculty members join and leave our Board. Most are very willing at first, until they realize that most retention issues are not related to academics. I can recall numerous retention meetings where we spent most of the time talking about financial, social fit, or other issues that had no direct connection to academics. During these meetings the faculty members were not engaged in the conversation. I can only surmise that is when they realized their time would be better spent working on tasks directly related to their specific field of expertise. Several years ago, a faculty member who was attending our meetings, stopped me afterward and said he needed to step down from the committee. This was following a meeting that primarily focused on students who leave for disciplinary/legal issues, our strike policy, and other non-academic items. He went on to say he now has a better understanding of retention at the University and we should be commended for our efforts, but he could not offer much assistance and had other things to work on directly related to his home department. We currently have three good faculty members on our Board. I am hopeful they will continue to serve, as their presence is an asset.

Institutional Research and Effective Planning: This person is an absolute must for any retention group. During our early years as the Retention Task Force and later the Retention Steering Committee, the Institutional Research (IR) representative could have spent most of her day working on retention-related tasks. Although we have come a long way in that much of our needed data is automated, thanks to IR's work over the years, this person continues to provide information that we use in all of our retention efforts. It seems each year we continue to increase our retention data and reporting. Most recently our IR representative introduced Tableau to our retention efforts. This system has enabled numerous campus professionals to access their own retention data without having to make a request to IR. We strive for all our proposed initiatives, decisions, and reports to University leadership to be data-driven. I can say with 100% confidence that our IR representative has ensured we are living up to this standard.

Assistant Provost/Registrar: Support from the Office of the Provost or another top leadership unit on campus is paramount in successful retention efforts. I have already highlighted this key factor in Initiative 1, but want to reiterate its importance. Having the assistant provost or the registrar on a retention group is ideal. Our board is fortunate in that our assistant provost is also the University's Registrar. From offering a perspective with the provost's primary objectives in mind, to explaining the "how" and "why" of various University policies as only the Registrar can, I am grateful this person is on our Board.

Center for Student Success and First-Year Experience (Associate Director): In my opinion successful first-year experience programs are valuable contributors to student success and persistence. At our University, a majority of first-year experience programs are housed in the Center for Student Success and First-Year Experience. Therefore, including the administrator who oversees these programs has been significant to our Board. Although we offer a robust collection of first-year experience programming, our largest and most widely known is our EDHE 105 "The First-Year Experience" course. EDHE 105 is an optional, letter-graded, three credit-hour course, which counts as an elective for nearly every degree. Some 70% of the freshman cohort chooses to take this course that helps them make the successful transition from high school senior to college freshman. From content in the course (e.g., time management, college study skills, campus resources) to utilizing the EDHE 105 instructors as front-line retention officers, I firmly recommend that a first-year experience administrator be included in everyone's group who oversees retention.

Center for Student Success and First-Year Experience (Assistant Director-Retention): This position was briefly addressed in Initiative 2, as one of the key people who think about student retention on a daily basis. Our Assistant Director-Retention does have some daily retention related responsibilities such as overseeing our First-Year Attendance Based Initiative, reviewing daily dropped-schedule reports and making contact with those freshmen who dropped, and creating retention-related reports which are sent to various campus constitutes. Other than our Institutional Research representative, this person is our primary source for retention data. Furthermore, by them having the technical skill set and commitment to freshman retention, we are extremely efficient and timely in our efforts, as we do not have to constantly ask Institutional Research for information. Our assistant director-retention works closely with Information Technology and Institutional Research not only on behalf of the Retention Advisory Board, but also in her day-to-day functions within the Center for Student Success and First-Year Experience.

Center for Student Success and First-Year Experience (Assistant Director-Academic Support Programs): One representative on the Board who has a tremendous opportunity to impact freshman retention is our assistant director-academic support programs. Each year some 10% of the University's freshman cohort are placed on academic probation (less than a 2.0 GPA) after the fall semester. These students are required to take EDHE 101 "Academic Skills for College." These at-risk students are one semester away from being placed on academic suspension, thus this mandatory course provides us with the opportunity to support a significant number of potential drop-outs. This representative also oversees our Contractual Readmission Program (CRP) where students who go on academic suspension have the opportunity to return to the University without having to sit out a semester. Academically suspended students must apply to participate in CRP. Once accepted, the students agree to fulfill all program requirements, which include: consenting to a structured schedule, meeting weekly with an academic mentor, completing weekly study hours, and complying with other student support components. The previously mentioned initiatives are considered reactive, based on student academic performance. The assistant director-academic support programs also oversees proactive initiatives, such as academic consultations, Do It Yourself (DIY) Workshops, and peer mentor training.

Chemistry-faculty: Similar to my thoughts on our faculty member from Education, we tremendously value this person as part of our Board. Her input from a faculty perspective is always welcomed and even encouraged. Furthermore, she has been able to

RAB member Dr. Kerri Scott lecturing to a chemistry class

gauge other faculty members regarding various retention-related issues and report back to the board. This person has been an advocate of academic support programs that can help freshmen do well during their first year at the University. She was very involved in the Chemistry parachute program, which allows students who are struggling in General Chemistry (Chem 105) after the first exam to enroll in the slower paced Chemical Concepts (Chem 101). Rather than taking a poor grade in Chem 105 the students who opt to "drop down" can avoid a failing grade while getting more experience with what it takes to be successful in Chem 105. This parachute option has helped numerous students since its inception several years ago.

Dean of Students: The Dean of Students representative is relatively new to our Board. The Dean of Students has oversight of several units on campus that can have an impact on freshman retention. The University of Mississippi has a strong Greek community. During fall Rush many freshmen believe joining a Greek organization is essential to their college experience. For most who participate this is a very rewarding experience. However, from a retention perspective we do have some freshmen each year who leave the University citing a negative experience with Rush/Greek organization. The Dean of Students offers insight to this issue, as well as welcomes our input on ways to make improvements, such as seeking our input on the most ideal dates for rush. One other very important unit this person oversees is the Office of Conflict Resolution. Unfortunately, we have freshmen who make poor decisions and are subject to being suspended from the University for disciplinary issues. The Dean of Students welcomes our feedback regarding this issue and explains various policies in which we may have questions. Additionally, we are aware that freshmen who make a connection to the University are more likely to persist than their peers who do not. This representative oversees all campus organizations, so her assistance in helping freshmen get connected is appreciated.

Luckyday Program: This is one of the more unique positions on our Board. Luckyday is a competitive scholarship-supported program for Mississippi residents. Each year the program admits 75 new freshmen into the program. These freshmen are required to live in the Luckyday Residential College, enroll in EDHE 105, and participate in various support/community-building activities designed by Luckyday staff members. Additionally, Luckyday offers programs and support to upperclassmen who receive the scholarship. Luckyday freshmen are retained at higher levels than the overall freshman cohort. The ideas and feedback the Luckyday representative provides the Board are helpful. Even though Luckyday is competitive entry and offers scholarship money, some of their programs and support services can be adapted to other groups on campus. Finally, the Luckyday representative plays a significant role in the training and professional development for all EDHE 105 & 305 instructors (some 150 people). This training is vital in our efforts to support students as they persist at the University.

Center for Inclusion and Cross Cultural Engagement: The Center for Inclusion and Cross Cultural Engagement (CICCE) was established at the University in 2014. The Board was pleased to have the CICCE director join our group almost immediately after the Center's opening. Historically, the persistence of minority freshmen lags behind their Caucasian peers. Most recent fall-to-fall retention data indicated the gap was slightly over 3% (86.9% vs. 83.8%) for the 2014 Freshman Cohort. In the short time the CICCE representative has been on our Board, we have seen new initiatives implemented to support the University's minority students. From peer mentoring to an increase in social and educational opportunities for minority students, the CICCE is an instrumental component in our retention efforts. As the CICCE continues to expand its services, programs, and resources, I am excited about the wonderful opportunities it will afford our students, and the impact it will have on student persistence.

Developmental Studies: Developmental Studies serves a significant segment of our freshman cohort. Each year the University of Mississippi enrolls a number of freshmen who are required to enroll in developmental English, reading, or math based on sub-scores on their standardized tests. As our non-residents' admission requirements have increased over the last three years, the number of non-residents needing developmental courses has decreased. However, admission standards for Mississippi residents are minimal, thus we do have numerous in-state freshmen who are required to enroll in developmental courses. Unfortunately, retention data indicates that freshmen, who are required to enroll in developmental courses, persist at lower levels than their peers, who are not mandated to take the courses. The Developmental Studies representative on our Board is aware of these statistics and continues to try to improve retention rates for this population. He gives regular updates on their efforts, while offering and seeking input regarding the role of developmental studies in our retention efforts.

Responsibilities of the Retention Advisory Board

The role and responsibilities of the Retention Advisory Board have changed over the years. However, the ultimate goal of helping all freshmen at the University of Mississippi endure from year one to year two has remained constant. Members of the Board are expected to attend monthly meetings, respond to inquiries sent to our retention e-mail list, generate reports as needed, represent their area(s) of oversight, and engage in other retention-related responsibilities. Each member is unique in what he/she brings to the group. These singular perspectives, abilities, and areas of oversight are strengths of our Board and have been critical to our record-setting retention efforts over the last several years.

When the retention group was first created many of the essential tasks were performed by a committee approach. Although this new approach was better than nothing, it was not always efficient, as committee members had full-time campus positions and were not always able to dedicate the necessary time to retention activities. However, the initial policies, procedures, and initiatives that this group implemented, continue to be vital in today's efforts. The big distinction is that we are now much more efficient in our efforts. For example, when we would work on "no-schedule" freshmen (i.e., freshmen who had not created a class schedule after priority registration), it could take several days and multiple committee members to begin identification and contact efforts. Today, our assistant director-retention in the Center for Student Success and First-Year Experience can quickly identify freshmen who have not registered and share their contact information with various campus colleagues in a matter of hours. The quick turnaround in identification and contact efforts has made a difference in assisting our freshmen identify barriers that may have prevented them from returning to the University.

Another example is when the old committee began an initiative to contact freshmen with low mid-term grades. Although we discussed the initiative at our monthly meeting, we were unable to enact it immediately. Institutional Research had to explore ways to extract the data. Then we needed to identify who would receive the data and what type of intervention could be made. Now it is an automated process where academic advisors, EDHE 105 instructors, and others receive the information a few days after mid-term grades have been submitted. Again, the groundwork the committee conducted years ago was valuable in establishing a great intervention, and today we continue to use the program in an efficient support effort.

With many of the essential tasks now automated and the processes and players fine-tuned, the current Retention Advisory Board spends more time focusing on big-picture ideas, revising policies to be more retention-friendly, and creating new programs. We have several years of data related to why freshmen leave the University and have streamlined our collection efforts; what began with campus representatives sharing multiple spreadsheets has grown into a tailored online retention tool where notes are easily shared and reasons for leaving are updated regularly. Furthermore, this tool allows us to identify students as "Do not contact;" this alerts campus professionals that they have informed someone they are not returning. Based on this data, the Board knows that the top three reasons freshmen cite for leaving the University are based on (a) distance from home; (b) financial concerns; and (c) social fit. The Board actively discusses these issues, and continues to explore solutions.

Another advantage to not getting bogged down in day-to-day operations is the ability to identify University policies and procedures that could be more retention-friendly. Given that one of the most frequent responses students give for not persisting is related to financial concerns, the Board has worked with Finance and Administration. Some requests have been successful, while others have not. One successful initiative occurs after priority registration has ended. The Bursar agrees to temporarily remove bursar holds for freshmen who owe $400 or less. This is very beneficial as it affects approximately 100-200 freshmen each semester. These students

The top three reasons freshmen cite for leaving the University are based on (a) distance from home; (b) financial concerns; and (c) social fit.

will then have the ability to register while most classes are still available. However, not all proposals are accepted. Each semester we see freshmen who owe thousands of dollars after priority registration has ended. We have asked the Bursar to create and promote a formalized payment plan. Under such a plan, students and their families can make payments as often as they like, but it is not formalized, and students are not encouraged to sign up for a payment plan at the beginning of the semester. It is frustrating, from a retention perspective, to hear from freshmen or their parents that the experience has been great, and that they would love to return, but owing several thousand dollars in tuition and fees, with no plan to pay it off usually forces students to leave the University. Other policies and procedures in which the Board has been successful in implementing change has been with EDHE 105, EDHE 101, August Orientation attendees, financial support, military documentation, and Student Housing. Unfortunately, we also have advocated for change in other areas, but have not had the same type of success. Some of these examples include different penalties for holds, a later drop date, and fraternity/sorority recruitment. The Board has made tremendous headway in the University's retention efforts, and will continue to explore all possibilities in making sure our freshmen are successful, satisfied, and retained.

Opportunities for the Future

The future is bright for the Retention Advisory Board at The University of Mississippi. Over the last three freshman cohorts (2012-2014) when the Center for Student Success and First-Year Experience began overseeing much of the day-to-day freshman retention operations, thus allowing the Retention Advisory Committee to become the new Retention Advisory Board, the University has set retention records. This model of allowing one center to focus on daily operations, while an advisory board looks at big-picture issues, has been effective for us. For the record, I changed the retention group from committee to board in 2013 when I took over as chair. I viewed the term "committee" to be more temporary; by changing to "board" it is more permanent, and we know retention is going to be a lasting issue that institutions will face. Additionally, I wanted to move the committee in a different direction from where everyone had individual responsibilities related to retention tasks. The new Center could oversee those tasks; thus, changing the group to a board allowed members to bring unique perspectives to broad view retention discussions, and members each had an area of oversight on campus where they could make an impact.

Although we have made a significant impact on freshman retention, I know there is still room to improve. Opportunities to better our efforts are abundant if we all continue to pull the rope in the same direction. By our Board's persistence of reviewing retention data and working with campus colleagues who can assist in our mission, we look forward to what the future holds. For example, each semester we know we will lose a significant number of freshmen who cite "financial concerns" as their primary reason for departure. Thus far we have been unsuccessful in convincing the Bursar to develop and promote a formalized payment plan. We will continue to explore that initiative, but in the meantime, Finan-

The Retention Advisory Board discusses all aspects that affect student persistence.

cial Aid has increased their outreach in educating prospective students and parents/guardians on the cost of attendance at the University of Mississippi. Financial Aid's most recent initiative presents Orientation students and their parents/guardians a worksheet related to cost of attendance. With over 50% of the freshman cohort being non-residents, who must pay the additional non-resident fee, it is critical to our retention efforts that new students and parents/guardians have a plan to pay for their college education at the University of Mississippi. Additionally, Financial Aid is constantly investigating other options on how to educate new students and parents regarding the cost of attendance.

There are a few other possibilities that come to mind when thinking about retention opportunities in the short-term future. During fall semesters, it is not uncommon for a handful of new freshmen to withdraw from the University immediately following fraternity and sorority recruitment. We are aware of freshmen who drop and we make contact with them on a daily basis. The students who leave the University during the days following recruitment, almost always indicate they did not receive a bid or did not receive the bid they wanted from a specific group. Additionally, other freshmen may stay to finish the semester, but decide not to return after winter break citing a bad experience with a fraternity, sorority, or the recruitment experience. Ongoing discussions occur within the Board and with other campus leaders regarding this issue also have centered on ideal dates of recruitment to targeted outreach for those who drop out of recruitment or do not receive a bid.

Finally, we have freshmen tell us they are not returning because it was not a good social fit or they preferred to go to a school closer to home. Although there may be other key factors that students fail to mention, and that we have little control over (e.g., cheaper to go to school in-state, boyfriend/girlfriend back home, etc.), we know that helping students make connections is key to them persisting at the University. With many freshmen being non-residents, we attempted to help some of the freshmen from greater distances get connected to each other by hosting regional/state freshman meet and greets. We picked seven regions/states and invited all freshmen from those states to a meet-and-greet event, where these new freshmen could find a smaller group of people who are from their area of the country. Next year, with the Board's support, we are continuing the meet-and-greets, but also adding social media groups for new freshmen, based on geographic location. We are hopeful that helping new freshmen connect with peers from the same area, as well as including faculty and staff from those same areas, can help overcome negative feelings of isolation and social fit as retention-related barriers. As long as the Retention Advisory Board maintains its focus on helping freshmen persist, we will have numerous opportunities to explore initiatives while assisting our students through their higher education journey.

Question:

Would your retention efforts do better under a committee or board?

RETENTION ADVISORY BOARD

Does your institution currently have a group who oversees retention efforts?

Members/campus titles:

_____

_____

_____

_____

_____

Examples of their work:

_____

_____

_____

_____

_____

Brainstorm ways to create a group who oversees retention. If a group already exists, list some ways the group can increase their productivity (e.g., adding new members, creating new initiatives, exploring the effectiveness of programs already in existence, etc.).

_____

_____

_____

_____

_____

_____

_____

Interview

Leslie Banahan
Assistant Vice Chancellor for Student Affairs

Describe your role in the University's retention efforts.

As assistant vice chancellor for student affairs, I have worked with retention initiatives for more than 20 years. I serve on the Retention Advisory Board and have oversight of a number of departments that play critical roles in student success and retention: Center for Student Success and First-Year Experience, University Counseling Center, Student Disability Services, University Health Services, Career Center, and Campus Recreation.

In your opinion, what are some of the most effective retention strategies at the University?

One of our key strategies is the commitment and support of our Office of Institutional Research Effectiveness and Planning. Members of this office serve on our advisory board and provide daily metrics that help us track retention and respond quickly to students who need assistance to stay in school and/or be academically successful.

Since you became involved in the University's retention efforts, describe some changes you have observed.

The biggest change I have seen is the assignment of retention to one, specific office. Too often, retention is the responsibility of everyone and no one. To truly "move the needle" on retention, one or more faculty/staff members need to have both the responsibility and authority to engage campus colleagues in retention efforts. Increasing retention requires a commitment of resources, both financial and personnel. Successful retention needs daily attention by one or more people. It is not seasonal work!

Where do you see retention efforts going in the short term? Long term?

I think retention efforts will rely more and more on data, drilling down to determine who stays, who goes, who is successful. The more specific the data, the better we can address the needs of students. Long term, I hope our institution will fund one or more data analysts dedicated full-time to retention.

What advice would you give other institutions regarding their retention efforts?

Our success is due in large part to the partnerships we have created with colleagues across campus. Find those faculty and staff who are passionate about student success and ask them to serve on your steering committee or advisory board. Engage your chief academic officer in retention discussions, and ask for his/her support. Tap into the campus resources you need, especially institutional research. Track retention daily, and share this information broadly. Finally, make it personal. Engage with students who leave your institution; find out why they left and offer support if they wish to return. Follow up with these students. Analyze the reasons students give for leaving; share this information with the departments that need to know of students' negative experiences so changes can be implemented.

INITIATIVE 4
DATA COMMITMENT

The need for accurate and timely data is paramount to good retention programs. Everyone wants to make "data-driven decisions," but what happens if the needed data is unavailable or cannot be delivered in a timely manner? Fortunately, at the University of Mississippi the Office of Institutional Research, Effectiveness, and Planning (IREP) is very supportive of our retention efforts. Not only does the interim director serve on our Retention Advisory Board, and provide data to our retention group, this person also assists other campus departments in collecting retention-related data. Furthermore, the speed at which requests are met must be commended. Colleagues at other institutions are amazed at how quickly our IREP office fulfills retention requests. In addition to IREP the Center for Student Success and First Year Experience's assistant director-retention is a valuable asset regarding data dissemination. This person has taken on many of the reports and data requests that previously went to IREP. Having someone who thinks about retention on a daily basis, and is able to create, analyze, and distribute retention data is a key component to our success. Our campus community should also be acknowledged in their support of requesting, analyzing, and acting upon data that has the potential to impact retention. Retention data can come in a variety of forms such as by academic major, special program, at-risk factors, etc. Therefore, campus colleagues who have oversight of various groups of students and strive to use data in their retention efforts are greatly appreciated. I can confidently state that without our commitment to collecting and providing quality retention data, we would not have achieved the significant increases in retention rates over the past several years.

Former IREP Director Mary Harrington sharing data on student success outcomes

Institutional Research, Effectiveness, and Planning

The Office of Institutional Research, Effectiveness, and Planning (IREP) has been heavily involved in the University of Mississippi's retention efforts since the 2008 Retention Task Force was established. Not only did IREP provide needed data to that group, it has continued to go above and beyond in the name of student retention. As the University further explores all facets related to student retention, IREP will remain a vital component in our retention efforts.

In the early years IREP, which in 2008 was launched as Institutional Research, created reports from scratch. Many of these reports could take several weeks to create, as this was the first time IREP was asked for specific data. Furthermore, the University was just beginning its vast emphasis on freshman retention, so almost everyone understood when a data request was not immediately able to be fulfilled. Many of the projects took hours, days, and even weeks for our IREP colleagues to establish the request's parameters, create the report, analyze the data, and distribute the information. Please keep in mind that retention data requests were among numerous other campus requests, and depending on who made the request, could affect its place on the priority scale. Fortunately, the initial Retention Task Force had the backing of the provost and an IREP representative as part of the group, so most of our requests were a top prior-

> IREP has continued to go above and beyond in the name of student retention.

ity. Based on my own recollection and review of Retention Task Force meeting minutes, the first large data extraction focused on many specific retention variables such as residency, gender, ethnicity, socioeconomic status, major, to name a few. This information allowed subcommittees to make recommendations based on data that identified the University's freshmen who were least likely to persist. Once the Retention Task Force was condensed to the Retention Steering Committee, our requests to IREP changed. Once we were able identify specific populations who were at risk of leaving the University, the group's leadership knew they needed to identify a smaller group who could recommend and implement specific strategies to impact retention.

After the retention group transformed from the Retention Task Force to a smaller Retention Steering Committee, which included an IREP representative, we were able to identify specific requests, which could make an instant impact. In addition to meeting the immediate needs, the group was able to focus on comprehensive issues that addressed the current cohort, as well as future new freshmen. Some of these targeted efforts included (a) freshmen who had not registered for the upcoming semester after priority registration had occurred; (b) courses with the highest D, F, and W rates; (c) freshmen who had holds, which prevented registration; (d) financial balances of freshmen who had yet to register after priority registration; and (e) other measurable attributes based on the Committee's recommendations. Although we were grateful for the data, interventions were not as imminent as they are today. It was common practice for the Committee to discuss an issue, ask IREP for the data, wait for IREP to discuss the data at the next meeting, and then anticipate the Committee making a recommendation based on data and discussion. Unfortunately, from a timeless perspective, this cycle could take up to three months, which did not allow for an immediate outcome from the committee.

Today many of our procedures for acquiring data are automated. We know what is needed and the time frame in which this data is best utilized.

Additionally, IREP began using a new system, Tableau, in which users can pull retention data using numerous variables. Tableau allows for quick reporting and the ability to provide answers to leadership in minutes, and without having to trouble IREP to create a report. The newest benefit of Tableau is the linkage to our online retention tool. The ability to acquire useful retention data has never been easier. Furthermore, if additional information is needed, IREP is willing to help as they are not overburdened running retention reports like they were a few short years ago.

CENTER FOR STUDENT SUCCESS & FIRST-YEAR EXPERIENCE ASSISTANT DIRECTOR-RETENTION

Having an in-house data person is very beneficial. The Center for Student Success and First-Year Experience's (CSSFYE) assistant director-retention has not only eased the data demand on IREP, this person also allows us to have immediate access to needed data. My office is adjacent to this person. It is not uncommon for me to ask for a specific report or a needed number to answer a question from leadership on a daily basis. The report or my numbers are usually delivered within a matter of minutes. Furthermore, the assistant director-retention and I are able to brainstorm ideas while using her data as a guide. Last fall we decided to host meet- and-greets by regions/states for new freshmen. However, due to resources and staff we were only able to host seven. Therefore, we reviewed prior-year retention data on non-residents who left the University and cited "distance from home" or "social fit" as their primary reasons. We identified the states and regions that had the most students cite those reasons, and targeted them to be in our pilot initiative. After we planned the seven meet-and-greets, our assistant director-retention created a report to identify new freshmen from those areas. She used student information from summer orientation registration, as the freshman cohort was not solidified in our campus management system. We did not want to wait until after the 10th day of the semester (our official census date) to pull this data, as the meet-and-greets were held during the first two weeks of the semester. This swift data reporting helped us acquire the needed information quickly so we could help new freshmen from the most at-risk geographic areas get connected. We were able to invite these new freshmen to our event and send their parents/guardians an email about the gathering. Based on parent feedback I received, they were pleased we were hosting the events and keeping them in the loop.

Another great example of our assistant director-retention gathering and utilizing data in a timely fashion is her immediate interaction with freshmen who drop their schedules. In the past IREP would send us a weekly report which documented freshmen who dropped, their drop date, and contact information. Although these weekly reports were better than nothing, contacting the students several days after they had dropped was not ideal. Thanks to the hard work and dedication of our assistant director-retention, she runs a drop schedule report every morning and identifies every freshman who dropped during the last 24 hours. The instantaneous information she collects allows her to make contact with these students immediately.

I can recall numerous examples of freshmen who have dropped their schedules, but were contacted shortly thereafter and received assistance in addressing the primary barrier that caused them to drop. In many cases the success stories involve financial concerns. For example, freshmen may drop their fall schedule after priority registration believing they would lose their scholarships next year. Thanks to the instant contact from our assistant director-retention, this student can be informed of the scholarship appeal process, offered help with the appeal after final grades are released, and re-register for most of the classes they had on their schedule before dropping.

Another example includes freshmen who drop schedules because of a change in the family's ability to pay for the upcoming semester. Our retention efforts have addressed several freshmen over the years who did not believe they could afford to return to the University for a second year after the family's income had changed from year one to year two. This could be due to a death in the family, significant health issues to a parent/guardian, or loss of a job. Fortunately, our Office of Financial Aid is a tremendous ally in our retention efforts. If we learn of a freshman experiencing any of the aforementioned scenarios, Financial Aid will review the student's situation and assist when possible. Results vary, but it is not uncommon for a student to complete a new Free Application for Federal Student Aid (FASFA), be recommended for departmental scholarships, or awarded one-time retention funds to help them get through the unplanned financial difficulties. Although the second two options depend on how well the student performed academically, the University strives to keep all students who begin their education at the University, especially those who have proven they can do well academically. Without our assistant director-retention contacting these freshmen immediately after their schedule drop, they may have never been informed of the assistance we can provide, or it may have been too late if they were contacted after they had already made other educational plans.

I cannot overstate how valuable timely information is to our retention efforts. With IREP receiving data requests from across campus, the ability for our in-house person to generate, analyze, and disseminate retention information in a well-timed manner has been a key component to our record-setting numbers. The chart below provides a timeline containing the type of data report and the recipient(s) the CSSFYE assistant director-retention provides for our retention efforts:

Freshman Cohort: 2014

Month	Reports	Recipient(s)
August	Begin daily check to see if any students have dropped their fall schedule, reach out when necessary	Asst Director of Retention
September*	Beginning mid-month, weekly holds report - targeting financial holds in preparation for registration; continue daily checks for dropped fall schedules	Holds owners, cohort owners, and advisors
October	Continue weekly holds report as registration nears and daily checks for dropped fall schedules	Holds owners, cohort owners, and advisors
November	Continue weekly holds report and daily checks for dropped fall schedules; begin daily checks for added and then dropped spring schedules, reach out when necessary	Holds owners, cohort owners, advisors, housing, dean's offices
December	Holds reports continue through to winter break; CSS-FYE takes ownership of the cohort and helps any student	Holds owners, cohort owners, advisors, dean's offices
January	Weekly holds report continue after break through to the tenth day of class (census date)	Holds owners, CSS-FYE advisors
February	Begin daily check to see if students have dropped their spring schedule; beginning weekly holds report - targeting financial holds in preparation for registration	Holds owners, cohort owners, and advisors

March	Continue weekly holds report as registration nears and daily checks for dropped spring schedules	Holds owners, cohort owners, and advisors
April	Continue weekly holds report and daily checks for dropped spring schedules; begin daily checks for added and then dropped fall schedules, reach out when necessary	Holds owners, cohort owners, advisors, housing, dean's offices
May	Weekly holds reports continue through to finals week; CSSFYE takes ownership of cohort and helps any student	Holds owners, cohort owners, advisors, dean's offices
June	CSSFYE continues reaching out all summer to all cohort members; daily checks for dropped fall schedules, reach out when necessary	Holds owners, CSSFYE advisors
July	CSSFYE continues reaching out all summer to all cohort members; daily checks for dropped fall schedules, reach out when necessary	Holds owners, CSSFYE advisors
August	Finalize cohort by the census date to have a departure reason for all freshmen who do not have a schedule	Asst Director of Retention

After 10th day of the semester

CAMPUS COMMUNITY UTILIZING DATA IN RETENTION EFFORTS

Many people on our campus have heard me say that data is vital to our efforts, but unless we have the front-line professionals who can utilize it to positively impact retention, it is worthless. One could compare this to having a car, but no gas. We need both data and campus professionals who utilize the information to assist our students as they persist from year one to year two. As previously stated in this initiative, our IREP representative and the CSSFYE assistant director-retention provide data to numerous people who apply it to help freshmen stay enrolled in the University. Although many of the members of our Retention Advisory Board are campus administrators, they either personally utilize, or direct subordinates who use retention data.

EXAMPLES OF PUTTING RETENTION DATA TO USE

I could write an entire initiative containing examples of campus professionals utilizing data in our retention efforts. However, I will refrain, and only provide some of the key examples that come to mind:

No Schedule Reports: After priority registration is over, the CSSFYE's Assistant Director-Retention creates a variety of reports regarding freshman cohort members who have not registered. Three constitute groups, who immediately come to mind, who work with this data include academic advisors, special cohort owners, and the Department of Student Housing. These groups receive their lists and immediately begin making contact with their freshmen.

Most freshmen at the University of Mississippi are advised by professional academic advisors in the CSSFYE. The others are advised by professional advisors within their Schools or special programs; with the remaining few assigned to a faculty advisor. Our advising model has served us well when asking for assistance in communicating with the freshmen who have yet to register. The professional advisors in the CSSFYE, Schools, and special program have time to e-mail, call, and

Author's Advice

No schedule reports are easy to create and provide a quick view of students who need support.

text their freshmen to offer assistance with class registration. The few freshmen who have a faculty advisor all are under the College of Liberal Arts. Rather than ask the faculty to track down individual freshmen, an assistant to the dean contacts those students and offers assistance. These campus professionals have the knowledge of University resources that can address persistence barriers, and the care to stick with the students as they address one or more issues. Furthermore, the professional advisors are familiar with our online retention tool and can update the tool when students indicate they are not returning.

Similar to our academic advising model, many freshmen can be categorized into various special cohorts. Some of the special cohorts include: Honors College, Athletes, Ole Miss Opportunity, Developmental Studies, EDHE 105, EDHE 101, Luckyday, and Provost Scholars, to name a few. Campus professionals who oversee these special cohorts receive a list of the freshmen who have yet to register. On occasion, the cohort owner will attempt to make direct contact, but usually staff members who work for the cohort owner make the initial contact. The cohort owners and their staff members can perform similar functions as the academic advisors regarding contacting the no-schedule freshmen, offering assistance with persistence barriers, and documenting retention information in our online tool.

The Department of Student Housing is an excellent ally in our retention efforts. Once they receive their list, it is divided among the residence hall directors (RHDs). The RHDs then give the community assistants (CAs) a list of freshmen on their floor(s) who have yet to register. The CAs knock on doors in an attempt to gain information about why students have not registered. If students want to return, but have barriers, the students are given a campus professional's name and contact information who can help them with the issue. Additionally, the CA documents and shares student notes so we can continue to follow up with the student. This system provides worthwhile information that we may not have otherwise been able to gain from multiple calls, e-mails, and texts. We have found that some freshmen, who avoid contact attempts from campus professionals, are more willing to tell a peer CA why they have not registered or the reasons why they are not returning to the University.

Low Mid-Term Grades Reports: The University of Mississippi has a variety of resources designed to help students academically (e.g., tutoring, supplemental instruction, academic success workshops, academic consultations, etc.) However, many of these services are underutilized because students do not believe they need them until it is too late. One initiative that has worked well is to create low mid-term grade reports to share with campus colleagues. Mid-term grade reporting is required for all 100- and 200-level courses. After final grades are reported we identify all freshmen with two or more C-, D, or F grades; these students are then grouped by special cohort factors to form lists which campus professionals can use to contact the students with low grades. The Center for Student Success and First-Year Experience (CSSFYE) maintains academic support information that can be used by University staff as they discuss the low grades with the students and a plan of action for the remainder of the semester.

Three groups that use the low mid-term grades reports each semester are (a) academic advisors; (b) EDHE 101/105 instructors; and (c) special cohort owners. For CSSFYE professional advisors it has become routine to expect a low mid-term grade report for their advisees a few days after grades are released. Because the report's release coincides with academic advising for the upcoming semester, advisors already would have planned to have a one-on-one meeting with the students on the list. However, by receiving their lists, the advisors expedite the advising process by encouraging the low mid-term grades freshmen to come in for advising and have a conversation about their academic performance through the halfway point of the semester. If advisors had already seen freshmen on the list for advising, they contact them and ask the students to come back in to talk about their low mid-term grades. During the conversations, advisors can show students how to make appointments with the Writing Center, find math tutors, talk about study strategies, and address other issues.

Instructors who teach our courses designed to support first-year students (e.g., EDHE 101 and 105, DS 095, 096, 097, 098, and 099) also utilize the low mid-term grades reports. We can sort the reports so instructors can easily identify the freshmen in their section(s) with low grades. We ask that EDHE instructors meet individually with all their students a couple of times during the semester. Choosing to have one of the meetings has been beneficial, as the instructors can offer praise to those who have good grades at mid-term, while offering support to those that are on the low-grade report. The continuous interaction that the instructors have with their freshmen is a tremendous asset; unlike the advisor who encourages the student to take advantage of the campus resources, the instructor can follow up with the student before/after class, if necessary. Additionally, the relationships that instructors build with their students can often create a more trusting environment where the student will share additional information as to why the mid-term grades are low. It is not uncommon for students to share that they are homesick, have health issues or are depressed, as the reasons for their low grades. In these cases, additional academic support may not be necessary. Referrals to the appropriate campus department(s) and follow-up by the instructor may be a more effective remedy.

Special cohort owners such as FASTrack, Luckyday, student athletes, and Provost Scholars receive low mid-term grades reports for their freshmen. These owners or their staff already know which students are struggling. However, in the world of retention, we leave no stone unturned, thus sharing the lists in case one additional student can be impacted. Similar to academic advisors and first-year course instructors, the special cohort owners contact freshmen on their lists and offer assistance.

Identifying, contacting, and assisting freshmen with low mid-term grades is a vital component to our successful retention efforts. Offering academic resources is not enough. Campus professionals who have a connection to students with low grades need to go the extra mile in encouraging them to take advantage of both academic and non-academic resources. As previously mentioned, we are seeing an increase in students with low grades who have issues other than academic preparedness and motivation. These students need to be supported, but sending them to the Writing Center is not going to make their health issue or homesickness go away. Getting to know the struggling student and making the "appropriate" referral is vital to helping them be successful.

Holds Reports: Approximately one month prior to registration windows opening, the assistant director-retention creates reports including freshmen who have one or more holds. These reports are then shared with campus administrators whose department controls the hold. At the University of Mississippi any hold on a student's account will prevent him/her from registering for courses. Some examples of holds include:

> Academic Advisor: The student must meet with an academic advisor.
>
> Student Conduct: The student had a disciplinary issue and must get it resolved.
>
> Bursar/Accounts Receivable: The student owes money (e.g., tuition, parking ticket, etc.)
>
> Admissions: The student needs to submit something to Admissions (e.g., final transcript).
>
> Alcohol EDU: The student needs to complete both parts of this mandatory assessment.

We understand that a key component to being successful is for students to pick the times, teaching style/delivery model, location, etc. of their classes. If students cannot register when their windows open due to a hold, the likelihood of creating a schedule that is most conducive to academic success decreases. Therefore, we appreciate the holds owners contacting freshmen who have their hold and offering assistance with hold removal. Academic advisors also play a role in this initiative. During academic advising, the advisor will check the student's holds and list them at the top of the advising sheet. In the fall semester, EDHE 105 instructors are given a list of their students who have holds prior to registration. They explain the importance of getting all holds cleared and registering as soon as the registration window opens. It truly is a team effort to help our freshmen get their holds removed before priority registration begins.

Example of the number of freshmen who had holds one month prior to registration during the Spring 2016 semester

886	Accounts Receivable Holds
30	Bursar Holds
73	Housing Conduct Holds
1	Campus Recreation
80	Athlete Hold
1	Student Activity (related to Campus Recreation)
4	RebelAdeJ
3	RebelAdeB
3	Health Holds
1	AlcoholEdu
10	Conduct Holds
1	Conduct Suspension

Advisor Holds are not set until two weeks prior to registration.

Data Commitment

Think about the current ways your institution utilizes data in retention efforts.

Who is the primary person?

_____

_____

_____

_____

What does he/she provide and to whom?

_____

_____

_____

_____

How is this data utilized?

_____

_____

_____

_____

Brainstorm ways to further utilize data in your retention efforts.

_____

_____

_____

_____

_____

Interview

Tiffany Gregory-Ward, Mary Harrington, and Jill Stribling
Institutional Research Effectiveness and Planning

Describe your role in the University's retention efforts.

The Office of Institutional Research, Effectiveness, & Planning (IREP) has been involved even before the inaugural Retention Task Force was created. The office has provided a variety of data and information to help inform the countless amount of retention efforts throughout the years.

In your opinion, what are some of the most effective retention strategies at the University?

In our opinion, though it may be a little bias, is that data are critical to have to make an informed decision and to understand the opportunities where improvements can be made. We also think by having data available and getting a daily reports created a healthy competition between schools/colleges in terms of retention. It also seemed to generate more interest and ownership at the school/college level and showcased that retention is a campus wide effort not just a student affairs issue or an academic issue. It was everyone's issue.

Since you became involved in the University's retention efforts, describe some changes you have observed.

We have gone from providing retention data in an ad hoc manner or reactionary to including retention work in our daily work. Retention moved from a year over year issue to a daily issue where students are being served in a way that will impact their lives forever. Retention isn't just a number anymore. It's a campus-wide initiative. Lots of different offices saw that they could take concrete steps to impact retention, so it really brought people together around a common goal. And the University showed it was a priority by devoting resources where needed. The focus wasn't just on high-level initiatives; strategies were developed to help individual students. That required much more time, but people knew it was a priority so they got creative and involved.

Where do you see retention efforts going in the short term? Long term?

Short term – continue to look for ways we can help provide useful information quickly and effectively.

Long term – find ways we can transition from just looking at and focusing on the New Freshmen cohort to other cohorts at the university. Also utilizing more advanced methods of identifying at risk students so that the university can effectively intervene earlier to help more students succeed.

What advice would you give other institutions regarding their retention efforts?

Retention is a campus wide issue as well as an important issue in a day to day – not just semester to semester or year to year. Also, retention is not about a number, it is about all the individual lives that make up that number.

INITIATIVE 5
PROFESSIONAL ACADEMIC ADVISORS FOR FRESHMEN

I have been known to use the phrase "freshmen have more in common with being a freshman than fill-in-the-blank major." In other words, a new freshman is going to have more first year/new student adjustment issues than with accountancy, journalism, sociology, or other major related issues. Therefore, I feel our model of utilizing professional advisors to support "anything and everything freshman" works well. At the University of Mississippi, approximately 70% of the freshman cohort is advised in the Center for Student Success and First-Year Experience (CSSFYE) during their first year. Of the other 30%, most of them are advised by professional advisors within their school or special program. Only a very small number of freshmen are advised by faculty.

Professional Academic Advisors in the CSSFYE

As the director of the CSSFYE, and based on the fact that this information pertains to 70% of our freshman cohort, I am only going to focus on the efforts of our professional academic advisors in the CSSFYE.

History of Our Model

In 2011 the School of Applied Sciences (SAS) agreed to pilot a partnership with the Academic Support Center (ASC), which involved professional advisors in the ASC providing advisement and support to all first-year freshmen in the SAS. The professional advisors could address all facets related to being successful during the first year at the University. The advisors were equipped to work with the population on all academic and non-academic issues. During the pilot year, it was not uncommon for advisors to assist this group with financial concerns, roommate issues, social adjustments, and other non-academic barriers that could impact persistence. In addition to the new professional advisors, each department in the SAS provided freshmen faculty mentors so first-year students could have a faculty member with whom to address major specific issues such as research opportunities, careers, and graduate school. In addition to the professional advisors and freshmen faculty mentors, the ASC utilized other mechanisms to

The CSSFYE advises approximately 70% of the freshman cohort.

ensure success. Following summer orientation, the advisors wrote letters and sent e-mails to all new SAS freshmen. This allowed new SAS freshmen and their parents to begin interacting with their first-year advisor before the semester even began. The ASC and SAS hosted a meet-and-greet early in the semester. This event allowed new freshmen to meet their first-year advisor and their freshman faculty mentor. Additionally, the ASC Director sent monthly e-mails to SAS freshmen and their parents. The e-mails provided general information regarding University resources, important dates, and other helpful advice in navigating the first year. Creating a partnership among the ASC, SAS, new freshmen, and their parents was the goal of the total support system model.

The qualitative feedback was great, and anecdotally, we could give several examples of ASC advisors helping freshmen to not only persist, but also to be successful and satisfied with their first-year experience. However, we knew the ultimate measure of success would be freshman fall-to-fall retention rates. We were pleased to see that after one year in the new system, the SAS increased from 82.3% for the 2010 cohort to 87.2% (+4.9%) for the 2011 cohort. In previous years the SAS finished in the middle to lower tier of all schools/college in freshmen retention. After the first year in the new model, the SAS was in the upper tier. The only significant change that occurred was the advising model, which utilized professional advisors offering more support to their first-year freshmen.

In 2012, after seeing the positive increase in freshman retention from the SAS and hearing excellent reviews from the SAS Dean, the School of Business Administration and the College of Liberal Arts decided to take advantage of the ASC offer. These were the largest academic school and college on campus. With the provost's full support, the ASC was allowed to hire four new professional academic advisors, and acquire new space in the Student Services building. The ASC envisioned using the same model that worked so well for the SAS. However, as with most schools and colleges within a university, everyone has their own nuances and the ASC had to compromise in order to make the new partnerships beneficial to everyone.

The School of Business (SB) was easy to work with, as they requested only some minor changes. During early partnership discussions the SB made it clear it was not interested in utilizing freshmen faculty mentors. However, they were agreeable to a designated dean's office representative who could work with freshmen on SB specific issues. Although we highly valued the mentor role with Applied Sciences, we understood SB's rationale and agreed to the change. Additionally, the SB organized their own meet-and-greets, which took place over four days early in the semester. ASC advisors and the director attended and spoke at all events. All other support services for SB freshmen followed the Applied Sciences model from the previous year.

When final 2012 freshman cohort numbers were released in early fall 2013, we were excited to see the SB increased from 80.3% to 87.5% (+7.2%) from the prior year. The SB had always been one of the largest schools, and increasing their retention rate by 7.2% in just one year was an outstanding accomplishment. This achievement was further evidence that employing professional advisors, who could address both academic and non-academic issues related to being successful during the first year, was the ideal model to help our freshmen be successful, satisfied, and retained at record levels.

The College of Liberal Arts (CLA) is the largest academic school/college at the University of Mississippi. When the CLA Dean approached the ASC about partnering to advise and support their freshmen, we were overjoyed. The CLA appreciated what we were able to accomplish with Applied Sciences, but wanted to allow each CLA department to determine the best model that would address their specific needs. After the ASC director and the assistant/associate CLA deans met to determine possible options, the CLA dean gave each department chair three choices: (a) Continue with the standard model of department faculty advising freshmen; (b) Utilize an ASC advisor-only model; (c) Participate in a professional advisor and freshman faculty mentor model. Most of the small departments (Art, Music, Philosophy, etc.) opted to keep the faculty-only model. Several of the classic Liberal Arts departments (Psychology, Sociology, English, etc.) chose to utilize the professional advisor only model. The larger departments (Biology, Chemistry, etc.) decided to use the professional advisor and freshman faculty-mentor model. Additionally, forensic chemistry, which is within the chemistry department, requested an additional role. Freshman faculty mentor wanted a mandatory advising session with each mentee.

All support initiatives such as the meet-and-greet, proactive communication, the majors fair, and other programming similar to Applied Sciences, were utilized in the partnership. The ASC staff and the CLA were in agreement that this partnership was beneficial to everyone. The ASC was able to support more freshman cohort members, while the CLA faculty were able to devote more time to upperclassman and graduate students in their respective fields. Final 2012 Cohort numbers which were released in fall 2013 indicated that CLA increased from 77.6% to 82.8% (+5.2%) from the prior year. The positive outcomes benefited the ASC, CLA, freshmen, and the entire University. Top campus administrators had now taken notice of what professional academic advisors for freshmen can accomplish when given appropriate support and resources.

With the three largest schools and college praising the work of the ASC professional advisors, as well as the retention data that supports their efforts, the provost's office began to strategically look at other schools that could benefit from a partnership with the ASC. Two new schools established partnerships with the ASC during summer 2013. The partnerships with the Schools of Engineering and Accountancy would begin during Fall 2013. However, reasons behind the schools choosing to partner were very different. Additionally, on July 2, 2013, the ASC officially became part of a larger, newly created unit known as the Center for Student Success and First-Year Experience (CSSFYE).

The School of Accountancy (SA) dean approached the CSSFYE director about a partnership to advise and support accountancy freshmen on the primary basis of relieving the advising responsibilities of the

Dean's Office. In the past, all accountancy majors were advised in the SA Dean's Office. The University of Mississippi had seen the freshman class grow by more than 37% in the past five years. Therefore, advising and support services for all SA undergraduate and graduate students were not as easily managed as they were five years ago. In the inaugural year of the partnership, the SA asked to use a similar model as that of the School of Business. The only addition the SA requested was that all freshmen who received Accountancy scholarships would also need to meet with a Dean's Office representative. Working with the University Information Technology, we were able to code this select group and create an accountancy hold on their accounts, which prevented registration until it is was removed. Unfortunately, retention did not increase after first-year partnering with the SA. However, several factors were well documented: The prior year SA set an all-time high retention record (95.4%), we began helping SA with problem freshmen the prior year, and SA had a significant increase (nearly 25%) in the number of freshmen during the partnering year. Even with the decrease, SA remained near the top of the retention list when compared to all University schools and colleges. Fortunately, during the second year of the partnership, the SA got back on track with a 93.7% fall to fall retention rate, which was the highest rate at the University.

Unlike all other partnering schools/college, the School of Engineering's (SE) partnership with the CSSFYE occurred differently. According to institutional data, the SE traditionally had one of the highest academically achieving freshman cohorts. Unfortunately, that did not translate into successful retention, as the SE

Quality academic advising can impact student success, satisfaction, and persistence.

was in the lower tier in freshmen persistence when compared to other University of Mississippi schools and colleges. The provost strongly encouraged the dean of engineering to partner with the CSSFYE in order to raise their freshman retention rate. After several meetings between the CSSFYE and the SE, a mutually-agreed upon model was created. This model differed from all other partnership models. The CSSFYE allowed the assistant director for advising to serve as the only engineering advisor. In addition to this unique change, the SE requested that each freshman be required to meet with a SE department faculty advisor. Therefore, SE freshmen had two holds and had to meet with two different people during the semester.

This partnership was watched closely throughout the entire year. When the fall-to-fall official retention numbers were released, everyone was pleased when the SE increased retention from the prior year, especially considering an increase in the number of freshmen. The primary factors that contributed to this positive increase were: (a) A dedicated advising professional in the CSSFYE who could address all freshman issues and was accountable for their retention number; (b) The proactive approach of helping some freshmen change majors who were never going to succeed in engineering; and (c) SE faculty who were still available to talk with freshmen about specific engineering issues (e.g., careers, graduate school, research), while the CSSFYE assisted with basic freshmen issues (e.g., first-year courses, financial concerns, social fit, campus involvement, homesickness, resources, etc…). Although this partnership came about via the provost's persuasion, both the CSSFYE and the SE would agree that it was a mutually beneficial arrangement that produced excellent outcomes.

Freshmen Retention Before and After Advising Partnerships

School/College	Before (Cohort Year)	After (Cohort Year)	Difference
Applied Sciences	82.3% (2010)	87.2% (2011)	4.9%
Business	80.3% (2011)	87.5% (2012)	7.2%
Liberal Arts	77.6% (2011)	82.8% (2012)	5.2%
Accountancy	95.4% (2012)	88.8% (2013)	-6.6%
Engineering	88.8% (2012)	89.2% (2013)	0.4%

Advisor Roles

CSSFYE academic advisors strive to treat every student as an individual. Establishing a trusting relationship with a campus professional is a key component to student persistence. Unfortunately, with advisor loads averaging 1:350, it can be difficult for academic advisors to spend much time with each advisee. This is especially true during priority registration. Our advisors are trained to understand that they must make the student feel comfortable with the advising process in order to achieve the maximum outcomes. Therefore, no matter if an advising session lasts 15 minutes or one hour, the advisor must foster a relationship with each advisee.

Establishing a trusting relationship with a campus professional is a key component to student persistence.

The CSSFYE begins advising six weeks before priority registration begins. This early advisement has both pros and cons. However, due to the large number of students assigned to each advisor, we must start earlier than all other advising units on campus. One benefit of starting early is that advisors can spend as much time as needed with individual students. Additionally, the early start allows advisors to not only discuss future courses, major and career plans, and other matters, but also current student issues that could be resolved early in the semester. By advisors getting to know students personally, they can talk about a variety of issues that can assist in student success, satisfaction, and persistence. This personal interaction is quite the contrast to advisors who do not have time for personal interaction and merely advise for next semester's classes. Unfortunately, students who wait to be advised until just before their windows open, do not benefit from as much personal interaction from our professional advisors, who see students back-to-back throughout the day. Therefore, we encourage all students to come in for advising well before priority registration.

One tremendous advantage to our academic advising model is that all our professional advisors comprehend the importance of freshman retention. These advisors have bought into and appreciate CSSFYE's main goal of helping students succeed. However, they also are cognizant of the bigger picture of the role they play in the University's retention efforts. For example, two years ago we changed our advising assignments from alphabetical to student major. This change increased the accountability for every advisor. No longer could we chalk up an advisor having a lower retention rate due to them having the letter "R" and it was a bad year for "R's." Now, we can better identify if an advisor, who advises a specific major, has a lower number each year, and can address the issue. The advisors

Academic advisors can be viewed as front-line retention professionals.

fully understand our intent when we send them lists of advisees who have holds, low mid-term grades, or who have not registered. They know the importance of acting on this information, not only for the students' benefit, but also the University's retention efforts.

I'm not sure if faculty advisors would have the time or even the willingness to contact students about retention information that is outside of their discipline. I appreciate the professional advisor model for freshmen and our retention data indicates it is working.

Most institutions offer campus resources (both academic and non-academic) to their students. However, many higher education professionals will admit that it can be difficult to get students to take advantage of such opportunities. Even though schools post flyers, send e-mails, and discuss the resources at orientation, many students simply are unwilling to take advantage of them. Professional advisors can participate in training regarding campus resources and stay up-to-date on institutional offerings. Therefore, when a student makes them aware of an issue, the advisors are knowledgeable about the various campus resources. I am proud of the fact that our professional advisors take this one step further. Rather than simply tell the students about a resource or give them an e-mail address, phone number, or office location, it is not uncommon for our advisors to refer the students to a specific person to contact, to make a phone call on the students' behalf, or to even walk the students to the appropriate office. Although many see the role of an academic advisor as a schedule builder, advisors have the opportunity to impact a student's experience much more. Connecting a student with a low math grade to a math tutor is great, but learning that a student is suffering from depression and getting that student to our counseling center can be even more important. Campus referrals are paramount in our retention efforts, as no one person is an expert on every student issue. Professional advisors for freshmen can be knowledgeable, stay up-to-date on new information, and provide the referrals that are needed in order to help our students succeed.

Another responsibility that I appreciate from our professional advisors is the outreach they are able to provide. Outreach to our freshmen can be both proactive and reactive. Regardless if the communication is before or after the fact, our advisors are in the loop on various opportunities for interaction. Some of our proactive advisor outreach initiatives include: welcome and introduction before the semester begins, congratulatory notes for good grades, and invitations to specific campus events and programs. Our advisors are assigned to send each new freshman who attended Summer Orientation a letter and e-mail introducing themselves. This communication arrives several weeks before the start of the semester so that new students may begin interacting with their advisor prior to the first day of class. Advisors also proactively reach out to students who earn good grades. At the end of each semester, advisors receive lists of their advisees who earned good grades. The advisors congratulate them and check in to see if the student has any questions or concerns about the upcoming semester. Additionally, our advisors make their advisees aware of various opportunities on campus. From meet-and-greets to freshman convocation, our advisors attempt to build open communication with their advisees while encouraging them to take advantage of pertinent campus opportunities. For example, during the spring semester, the advisors for undeclared freshmen encourage their advisees to take part in a free "Choosing Your Major" workshop. The advisors send emails and give out flyers during advising sessions. I believe their promotion of the event has helped the workshop achieve record participation recently.

> Campus referrals are paramount in our retention efforts.

Professional academic advisors also must be very responsive in their communication with students. Some of our reactive approaches include: low mid-term grade follow-up, no- schedule communication, and addressing holds. As mentioned in Initiative 4, our advisors receive lists of freshmen advisees who have two or more C-, D, or F grades at mid-term. The advisor reaches out to address the poor academic performance by the student. Advisors can not only offer information about academic support resources, but also potentially uncover issues that go beyond academics. In these cases, advisors can assist students in finding the appropriate solution for their issue. After priority registration is over, advisors are able to see which of their advisees have not registered for the upcoming semester. Advisors also can address students' barriers to registration. This communication also is useful if a student is not returning to the University. The advisor can update our online retention tool with notes they receive regarding a student's lack of persistence. When it comes to addressing holds, advisors can remind students about them during advising sessions, and follow up with them via e-mail if holds have not been removed. Whether the communication is proactive or reactive, professional advisors' interactions with advisees are a valuable piece of our student success and persistence efforts.

One common misconception is that academic advising equals schedule building. Undoubtedly, schedule building is a core component to advising; but as previously mentioned there is much more that should occur between the advisor and advisee to ensure a high quality experience. After other opportunities are taken advantage of in an advising session, advisors will then discuss future courses with each student. I see advising as a partnership between the advisor and the advisee. The advisor should be knowledgeable in the institution's policies, curricula, and resources. Being able to convey important academic information is an essential skill for academic advisors. It is important to note that the students should be active participants in the advising process. They need to be aware of their curriculum requirements and seek the advisors' input for questions that may arise. I believe that advisors who establish expectations with their advisees early on in the advising relationship, will not only teach students to be accountable for their education, but also will expedite the advising process by not having to explain course/curricula details to each and every student. As front-line campus professionals, academic advisors are given the opportunity to impact the students with whom they interact. Assisting students with course selection is important, but should be only a small piece in the advisor and advisee advising experience.

Freshmen Faculty Mentors

When the Center for Student Success and First-Year Experience (CSSFYE) partnered with the University's schools and college for freshman advising, all were given the opportunity to provide major-specific freshman faculty mentors. The School of Applied Sciences and some departments within the College of Liberal Arts chose to use the professional advisor in the CSSFYE combined with the major-specific freshman faculty mentor. In this model, the CSSFYE professional can address "anything and everything" freshman, while allowing the freshman faculty mentor to answer questions specifically about their major, career opportunities, research opportunities, internships, etc.

Students' professional advisor and freshman faculty mentor information can be found online in our campus management system. Additionally, when freshmen meet with their academic advisor in the fall semester, advisors list the mentor information on students' advising sheets. While meeting with an academic advisor is mandatory, seeing one's faculty mentor is not. Use of the freshman faculty mentor varies from semester to semester. Some students will make an appointment and visit with the mentor about major specific issues. Others e-mail the mentors questions. Because it is not required to meet with a faculty mentor, some students who might benefit from the interaction do not take advantage of the opportunity. I would like to see more freshmen communicate with their mentors and begin forming connections with faculty in their home department early in their academic career.

How active the freshman faculty mentors are, can be hit-and-miss. Over the years we have had some very involved mentors, but also some who were not. When we first asked department chairs to recommend mentors for their freshmen, we asked that the faculty members be very "freshman-friendly." After receiving the initial lists, there were several recommended mentors that we knew would do a good job. However, there were others on the list upon which we questioned department chairs.

We were not in a position to debate the choices, so we assigned mentors based on the department chairs' recommendations. At the beginning of the semester, we provide mentors with lists of new freshmen, expectations of a faculty mentor, and examples of ways they can interact with mentees within their major.

Faculty interaction has a tremendous opportunity to support an institution's retention efforts.

Over the past three years, I have received very positive feedback from both faculty mentors and their mentees. We recommend that the mentors e-mail their freshmen early in the semester. It is our hope that they introduce themselves and invite freshmen to contact them via e-mail or through office appointments. Some mentors on several occasions have gone above and beyond. I recall one freshman faculty mentor who invited mentees via e-mail to eat lunch with him in the freshman dining hall. I saw him later that semester and he said he had several freshmen come and introduce themselves while he was there. Another faculty mentor contacted all her mentees early in the semester and invited them to eat pizza one evening and fellowship with each other. While these are great examples of how mentors engage students in conversation at the start of the semester, most mentors send the initial e-mail and then wait to see if students take the next step in contacting them. I have heard from several students who have contacted their faculty mentor and received assistance. One student told her academic advisor about the faculty mentor offering her the opportunity to assist in his research. She was so excited to be involved in a research opportunity as a freshman. Another student relayed the story of the faculty mentor promoting the importance of doing internships. The freshman faculty mentor gave her contact information for companies who had recently offered internships to some of our students.

The summer after her freshman year, the student was successful in gaining an internship with one of the companies her mentor recommended. The professional advisor model combined with freshman faculty mentors has worked well at the University. I am hopeful that in the future we can get more students to interact with the mentor, encourage some mentors to be more active, and encourage other schools and departments to take advantage of this model.

PROFESSIONAL ACADEMIC ADVISORS FOR FRESHMEN

Think about the current academic advising model for freshmen.
Describe the model that is utilized (faculty, professional, mixed, etc.):

_____

_____

_____

_____

What are the expectations of advisors who assist freshmen?

_____

_____

_____

_____

Brainstorm ways to further include quality academic advising into freshman retention efforts.

_____

_____

_____

_____

_____

_____

Interview

Dr. Travis Hitchcock
CSSFYE Assistant Director-Academic Advising

Describe your role in the University's retention efforts.

I oversee the advising portion of the Center for Student Success and First-Year Experience (CSSFYE). Our academic advisors are responsible for advising approximately 70% of the freshman class. As academic advisors, we are often the first and primary official university representative that students turn to for questions and assistance in times of need. In fact, each student is compelled to meet with their academic advisor each semester. These meetings help us to forge relationships with our advisees.

At the conclusion of each semester, our academic advisors receive a list of all their advisees without a course schedule for the upcoming term. The academic advisors reach out to these students and asks whether they would like to return to the university. If the student would like to return, the academic advisor assesses the issue and makes an appropriate referral. If the student is not returning, the academic advisor determines the reason and makes a note in the university's online freshmen retention tool.

In your opinion, what are some of the most effective retention strategies at the University?

The most effective freshmen retention strategy at Ole Miss is the fact that nearly all freshmen are advised by professional advisors who are knowledgeable, available, and relatable.

Since you became involved in the University's retention efforts, describe some changes you have observed.

I've seen retention efforts change from being an afterthought and everybody's responsibility to a fully funded center where retention has become the primary responsibility of a handful of people. Retention efforts have changed from being reactive to proactive and is the motivating force behind every service the CSSFYE offers.

Where do you see retention efforts going in the short term? Long term?

In the short term, I see the university creating more programs and services to get students connected and "plugged-in" to campus life. Students seem less likely to leave if they feel like Ole Miss is their home.

In the long term, I think the university will continue to increase student admissions standards and will ultimately bring in more students who are better prepared to persist to graduation.

What advice would you give other institutions regarding their retention efforts?

Make retention the responsibility of a single office. Results are often motivated from people who take ownership of an outcome.

INITIATIVE 6
FIRST-YEAR EXPERIENCE COURSE

A first-year experience course can be an excellent tool to aid in student success, satisfaction, and persistence. Early in our Retention Steering Committee's work, we recommended revamping a first-year experience (FYE) course that was already in the catalog, but had not been taught in several years. The old course, US 101, was a mandatory one-hour credit, pass/fail class, taught primarily by faculty. However, it became apparent to the administration that both students and faculty were not overly eager to take or teach the course. Therefore, the University moved away from offering it. When the retention committee decided to bring the course back, we had to be very strategic in our plan of action. The committee knew we had to model the course after other universities' FYE courses that had proven to be successful. Some of our recommendations included making the course a three- credit-hour, letter-graded elective for nearly all majors, and able to be taught by any faculty or staff member who held at least a master's degree and cared about student success. And, most importantly, it would be optional for students. After several years, the revamped course, EDHE 105, has generated data that has measured student successes, won several awards, and been the subject of inquiries from colleagues around the country.

Overview of EDHE 105

Staffing

One of the most daunting aspects of a successful first-year experience (FYE) course is to find enough staff members who are (a) willing; (b) qualified; (c) knowledgeable; (d) devoted to our model; and (e) genuinely concerned about each new freshman in his/her course. Each aspect is very important. We strive to find individuals on campus who represent all five of the criteria. The Center for Student Success and First-Year Experience's associate director oversees all FYE initiatives, including EDHE 105. This person's oversight of staffing the course is very important. From offering just a few sections during the first year, to offering 126 sections during the fall of 2015 and teaching the course during summer sessions and spring semester, staffing EDHE 105 has become more complex. Although we have made our staffing model more efficient, tremendous section growth has increased the associate director's workload in finding enough quality instructors.

During the first several years of offering the course, we primarily relied on qualified campus professionals within the Division of Student Affairs to teach it. These individuals did not receive any personal compensation. However, their department was awarded a $500 honorarium. Many department heads allowed the instructors to use the $500 for professional development, but that was not always the case. Once the number of sections began to outpace the number of volunteers, though we knew we had a popular course (remember, it is optional), we also had a staffing problem on our hands. Fortunately, we were able to prove both academic and persistence success metrics to campus leadership when we submitted a new stipend model for instructors. Under the new model, staff members may use vacation hours and be paid $2,000 during the semester. Instructors who did not take the $2,000 stipend were still allowed to receive a $500 department honorarium. This funding model opened the door to many new campus colleagues who were now willing to teach. We now had doctoral students, faculty, retirees, and additional Student Affairs personnel inquiring about teaching the course. It is interesting to look back to the days when we had to call in favors to campus friends and ask them to teach; now, because of the expanded interest, we can be selective with our EDHE 105 instructors.

Course Content

As previously mentioned, we value instructor buy-in regarding course content. I have heard of other institutions that allow (or in some cases have no choice) their instructors to teach anything they want in the FYE course. This is not good for consistency in learning outcomes, accountability, and data collection. However, we do allow for some flexibility so instructors can put their own stamp on his/her section, but the core content must remain the same for all sections. We have a model syllabus, a required textbook written exclusively by campus professionals, year-round professional development, an e-mail listserv, recommended outside-of-class activities, and an end-of-semester assessment to ensure that all sections cover the same content. This content includes various transition issues, college study skills, time management, campus resources, health and wellness, financial literacy, and major/career exploration among other topics. Additionally, EDHE 105 supports learning opportunities outside the classroom. Some of these mandatory activities include freshman convocation, active shooter presentations by the University Police Department, and the library tour/education session. Other optional out-of-class activities include Career Center presentations, photo scavenger hunts for campus resources, campus historical tours, Writing Center presentations, and others.

Now that we have increased our campus partnerships by offering specific sections for various majors and special programs, we do allow for those sections to focus on issues that are pertinent to their students. For example, an Early Entry Pharmacy section may bring in guest speakers from the School of Pharmacy or focus some class discussions on what to expect while in pharmacy school; a section for undeclared freshmen may devote time to major exploration, invite career-related speakers, and offer various assessments from the Career Center. Regardless whether the section is limited to a special population, instructors must still incorporate all course requirements, in addition to the extra specialized content they choose to include. We have received positive feedback on the specialized sections from both students and instructors. Not only have these special sections provided departmental instructors for freshmen, thus assisting us in instructor staffing, the support from the academic schools and departments have increased. Each year we have more units requesting specialized sections, as administrators share their experiences with colleagues.

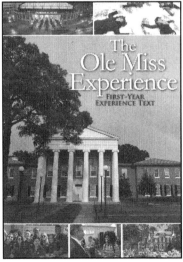

Using Your Own Textbook

There are numerous stock FYE textbooks that can be applied to any campus. In fact, our institution used these during the early years. However, it became apparent that to make the content more impactful, we needed the chapters within the textbook to focus specifically on the University of Mississippi. Our first step in creating our own textbook was to find a publisher. We were fortunate in that there was a publisher in Oxford, Mississippi who was willing to take on such a task and be very hands-on as we undertook this process. After identifying a publisher, a small advisory group had to determine appropriate book content, and select various campus experts who were willing to write chapters free of charge. Once all authors had been identified and accepted the responsibility, a meeting was convened with the publisher and on-campus editor to explain the purpose, author's role, deadlines, and answer any questions. I attended the first meeting, as I was asked to author the chapter on academic advising. This occurred while I was the Director of the Academic Support Center, a few years before I had oversight of the FYE unit, which now includes the EDHE 105 course. The group worked well together thanks to the publisher's recommendations and the on-campus editor who kept all authors on track.

Fortunately for EDHE 105, we have had the same publisher and on-campus editor every year since inception. This continuity has allowed for a very streamlined process, as we update the book's content on a yearly basis. Therefore, if University policies/procedures are updated, new programs are added, content needs to be changed, etc. the on-campus editor is on top of it. Furthermore, if

CSSFYE Associate Director, Dewey Knight, gives a historical tour to an EDHE 105 class.

an author leaves the University, or is no longer willing to participate, the on-campus editor can find a suitable replacement. Having our own textbook is very unique in that not only is the University-specific content accurate every year, we change the cover to make it original for each new freshman class. Although this is a wonderful practice to help our new freshmen transition into the University, it must be strategically coordinated and maintain a strict timeframe. Our on-campus editor sends all authors their chapters at the beginning of each spring semester and asks for updates. Authors have a couple of months to update information and send back to the editor. The editor then works with the publisher to ensure the new book will be ready for the fall semester. Additionally, we have added and removed chapters over the years based on recommendations or leadership asking us to address specific issues.

The current textbook is divided into five sections. The sections include College Survival, The University of Mississippi, Life Outside of the Classroom, Wellness, and What's Next in Your Life. The College Survival section focuses on topics such as getting off to a good start, time management, learning styles, reading college texts, and test-taking strategies, among others. The University of Mississippi section highlights the University's history, traditions, and civility. While discussing these chapters, I like to include a University historical tour. The third section, Life Outside of the Classroom, includes chapters such as campus involvement, diversity, campus safety, and money management. The fourth section, Wellness, addresses issues such as stress management, sexual health, substance abuse, and physical fitness. The final section, What's Next in Your Life, allows students to participate in career and major exploration. It even includes bonus material such as resume writing, successful interview tips, and information about our Career Center.

Gaining Student Buy-In

Although we know we have a good course, it is important to make sure new freshmen understand the course's benefit to them. Remember, our FYE course is optional. Therefore, if no students are willing to take it, the course will not be offered. Fortunately, we have seen demand for this optional elective increase every year since we began using the new model. I and the associate director tout the course's benefits during the welcome assemblies of orientation sessions. I speak briefly about the Center for Student Success and First-Year Experience (CSSFYE) and our associate director discusses the benefits of the course to new freshmen and their parents. We also include a two-page color course flyer in orientation bags. Orientation leaders and academic advisors are strong proponents of the course. Therefore, during formal sessions with academic advisors, or in casual conversations with orientation leaders, EDHE 105 is strongly encouraged for our new freshmen. Word-of-mouth also has been a valuable tool in our recruiting efforts. It seems many new freshmen already are familiar with the course thanks to siblings, friends, or other connections to older students who took EDHE 105. The CSSFYE advertises that we will always be able to find a seat for any new freshman who wants to take the course.

There are some circumstances in which we target identified at-risk freshmen for the course. We have years of data that suggest new freshmen who attend the August orientation (i.e., the last orientation prior to the start of the semester) have lower entering academic metrics, are likely first-generation college students, earn lower fall GPAs, are placed on academic probation, and persist at lower levels than their freshman peers, who attended an earlier orientation in May or June. Several years ago we began saving August orientation freshmen EDHE 105 seats in sections that meet between the hours of 10 a.m. and 2 p.m. We manually register these students into sections a few days prior to their orientation. We send students an e-mail about their registration and discuss the course at orientation. We inform them that they can drop the course if they wish, but we highly recommend they take it. Most stay in the course, as they understand the value and know that it is offered at a good time, when

Author's Advice

Speaking to new students and parents at Orientation is an effective way to promote FYE courses.

many of their other courses take place outside the ideal 10 a.m-2 p.m. time window. One other proactive initiative we employ is checking for new freshmen who are undeclared, business undeclared, or have a 22 or less on the ACT, and attended a summer orientation, but did not register for the course. A week prior to the beginning of the semester, we e-mail these students, inviting them to enroll in the course. Additionally, during the beginning of the second week of the semester, after students have had the opportunity to experience all their courses, we reach out to students who have yet to enroll and remind them about the class opportunity. Based on historical retention data, we know these students are at greater risk not to persist. Therefore, if we can get them connected to a campus professional who can monitor their progress, offer them academic skills,

Outside of class activities such as a behind-the-scenes tour of the Gertrude Ford Center for the Performing Arts can be excellent additions to FYE courses.

and discuss major/career exploration – all of which are a part of EDHE 105 – we feel there is a greater chance for them to be successful and remain at the University.

EDHE 105 Instructor's Role in Retention

EDHE 105 instructors are a tremendous asset to our retention efforts. As previously mentioned, we give careful consideration to whom we select to teach the course. Instructors must care about each individual student's success, not only in his/her course, but their overall well-being as they navigate the first semester of college. EDHE 105 instructors are unique in that they deliver academic content, but also can assist freshmen with non-academic issues. From the fall welcome meeting, in which all instructors are required to attend, to the individual professional development workshops offered throughout the year, we reinforce the notion that EDHE 105 instructors are an essential component to student success, satisfaction, and persistence.

Unlike some classes freshmen take during their first year at a large University, EDHE 105 is designed to enroll between 20-25 students per section. This small class environment combined with course content, activities, and open discussion, allows the students and instructors to form a connection. These close connections allow for trusting relationships in which the instructor can be seen as a dependable agent for the University. It is important for new students to feel as though they have a campus professional who can answer their questions and help them overcome potential persistence barriers. We require instructors to meet individually with each student at least twice during the semester. Additionally, students are welcome to contact their instructor at any time for guidance with both academic and non-academic issues. Students also are required to write in reflection journals throughout the semester. These journals offer instructors insight into how their students may be feeling about various issues during the first semester of college. I can think of numerous examples where students have written about potential retention risk-factors, such as homesickness or health issues, and the instructor was able to offer them assistance or make referrals to the appropriate campus department.

EDHE 105 instructors are heavily relied upon to be front-line retention professionals who implement various interventions based on alerts we distribute. Examples of informational warnings include low mid-term grades, holds, and no-schedule after priority registration has occurred. After mid-term grades are released, each instructor is given a list of students in their section who have two or more C-, D, or F grades. Most instructors have their first individual meeting with students around the time this list is distributed. During the meeting instructors can talk to students about courses, remind students of various campus resources, and develop an academic success plan for the remainder of the semester. If the distribution of low mid-term grades does not coincide with the meeting dates, instructors ask students on their lists to make appointments with them. Additionally, by instructors knowing which students are struggling in specific courses, they can frequently have casual conversations about progress in the course.

Before students are allowed to register for courses, they must have all holds cleared. Although students can see holds in their online student account, we know some students, especially new freshmen, do not check to see if they have any holds. Part of being a successful college student is registering for the appropriate courses when the registration window opens. EDHE 105 instructors stress the importance of timely registration. They

Question:

What is your ideal class size for FYE courses?

cover the chapter on academic advising a few weeks before registration begins. Having a conversation about meeting with your advisor to get your advisor hold removed can lead to reminders about taking care of other holds that will prevent registration. However, these conversations are not always enough to ensure that students are proactive; therefore, we provide each instructor with a list of students with holds. Instructors also receive information on how to remove the holds, which they can share with their students. Instructors usually discuss hold issues in private with students to avoid embarrassment with any undesirable holds. This initiative has been very valuable in getting the number of freshmen who have holds reduced prior to registration windows opening.

After all registration windows have opened, we provide instructors with a list of their students who have not registered for the upcoming semester. Instructors can work with students individually to address any issues that may be preventing registration. The relationships that have been established between the students and their instructors allow for instructors to gain information and offer assistance that may be useful in helping a student persist. Furthermore, the instructors are very knowledgeable of campus resources and can make referrals when necessary. If an instructor is unable to provide assistance, it is not uncommon for them to refer the student to me or the associate director. This enables us to take a personal interest in individual freshmen who are having issues that are not easily addressed. EDHE 105 instructors are viewed as an asset in the University's retention efforts. Even though the freshman cohort grows yearly, as do the number of EDHE 105 sections and instructors, the freshman retention rate continues to set records thanks to this caring group of campus professionals.

EDHE Course Outcomes

Edhe 105 is assessed in a variety of ways. Enrolled students and instructors are asked to evaluate the course at the end of each semester. Additionally, we work closely with the Office of Institutional Research Effectiveness and Planning to assess course outcomes regarding GPA, academic standing, and persistence. We even have the ability to view success metrics by sections so we know which instructors are the most effective. The tables below provide retention metrics from the past three freshman cohorts:

2013	Num	Avg ACT/SAT	Avg HS GPA	Not Retained	Retained
Did Not Finish EDHE 105	1,181	24.3	3.48	217 (18.4%)	964 (81.6%)
Finished EDHE 105	2,022	22.9	3.37	320 (15.8%)	1,702 (84.1%)
Total*	3,203	23.4	3.41	537 (16.8%)	2,666 (83.2%)

2014	Num	Avg ACT/SAT	Avg HS GPA	Not Retained	Retained
Did Not Finish EDHE 105	998	24.1	3.47	158 (15.8%)	840 (84.2%)
Finished EDHE 105	2,380	23.5	3.43	333 (14.0%)	2,047 (86.0%)
Total*	3,378	23.8	3.45	491 (14.5%)	2,887 (85.5%)

2015	Num	Avg ACT/SAT	Avg HS GPA	Not Retained	Retained
Did Not Finish EDHE 105	850	25.0	3.56	TBD	TBD
Finished EDHE 105	2,637	23.8	3.47	TBD	TBD
Total*	3,487	24.4	3.52		

*Excluding all Honors Students

First-Year Experience Course

Does your institution currently offer a first-year experience course? If so, consider the following components:

Who teaches the course?:

_____

_____

_____

_____

Topics covered:

_____

_____

_____

_____

Retention opportunities built into the course:

_____

_____

_____

_____

Brainstorm ways to create a first-year experience course. If a course is already in existence, consider opportunities to expand the role of the course/instructors in retention efforts.

_____

_____

_____

_____

INTERVIEW

Dewey Knight
CSSFYE Associate Director and Coordinator of EDHE 105

Describe your role in the University's retention efforts.

I have multiple roles within our retention efforts. First, I serve on the Retention Advisory Board which is the successor to the Retention Task Force and the Retention Steering Committee which were established to address retention at the University. As Associate Director of the Center for Student Success and First-Year Experience, I have responsibilities for first-year initiatives aimed at insuring a successful transition to the University and persistence at the University. These initiatives include two First Year Experience courses, EDHE 105 (First Year Experience course) and EDHE 305 (Transfer Student Experience course). I am also involved in various programming initiatives aimed at first year students including Fall Convocation, Common Reading Experience, Chancellor's Leadership course, and the Partnership for Student Success (Bridge program).

In your opinion, what are some of the most effective retention strategies at the University?

Some of the most effective retention strategies involve direct interaction with students. Our instructors in EDHE 105 and EDHE

305 act as advocates and counselors to their students. Our academic advising professionals work individually with each of their advisees to guide them to attainment of success and graduation completion. In general, I have to say, our total First-Year Experience program is vital to student's success and institutional goals with respect to retention, persistence, and graduation.

Since you became involved in the University's retention efforts, describe some changes you have observed.

Since my involvement in the University's retention efforts, I have seen a cultural sea change in the attitude of administrators and staff. There is a widespread acknowledgment of how important retention is to the University and her students at every level. The strong support of the Provost has been instrumental in raising retention as an institutional goal comparable to recruitment. Moving from a committee responsible for retention to a dedicated institutional unit with that responsibility is evidence of the change mentioned above.

Where do you see retention efforts going in the short term? Long term?

Retention will continue to be an institutional focus both short term and long term. In the current budgetary environment, retention is not an option. It is a requirement for institutional and student success.

What advice would you give other institutions regarding their retention efforts?

Institutions must make a commitment of resources necessary to insure retention goals are attained. In my opinion, an operational unit with administrative support and resources is vital for retention success.

INITIATIVE 7
PARENT INCLUSION

P arents can be a valuable ally when an institution aims to fully support students' success, satisfaction, and persistence. Students, especially freshmen, are going to communicate with trusted agents back home throughout their college experience. During the first several weeks of the semester, it is not uncommon for freshmen to admit that they communicate with a parent at least once a day. Additionally, I have witnessed students immediately calling or texting parents after leaving my class or following a meeting with their academic advisor. While some institutions have decided to hold onto an old school approach of asking parents to drop their student off, pay the tuition bill, but stay out of a student's university-related business, the University of Mississippi has adopted a

> It is important to be strategic in considering how parents are to be involved, as their involvement can greatly benefit retention efforts.

different tactic. Most college freshmen have been under their parents' watch for 18 years. We are not going to magically change a family dynamic by telling parents to pay the bill, but keep your nose out of your child's business. We want students and parents to have a good experience with our University. Therefore, we find it beneficial to create a balance between the new student being self-sufficient and the parent being involved from a distance.

I have three pieces of advice when it comes to including parents in an institution's efforts to support and retain students. The first is to fully understand why including parents is important to retention efforts. The second is to start the partnership early and remain consistent. The third piece of advice is to consider how you communicate with parents. An institution cannot say, "We want parents involved," but not actually have a plan to involve them. It is important to be strategic in considering how parents are to be involved, as their involvement can greatly benefit retention efforts.

UNDERSTANDING WHY INCLUDING
PARENTS IS IMPORTANT

As someone who went from limited involvement with parents to now having almost daily interaction with them, I can verify that the extra effort does make a difference. We have seen a significant increase in our freshman retention rates over the last several years. The timing of this increase corresponds with our change in philosophy to include parents in our student support efforts. We understand that students, especially freshmen, are going to communicate with their parents regarding collegiate issues, regardless if we recommend otherwise. Therefore, if we view parents as an ally and educate them on resources and other important information, which they can share with their students, we are increasing the odds that students will be informed. This is especially beneficial in situations where parents have influence over their freshmen. For example, if a freshman has a "D" in his/her WRIT 101 course at mid-term, the student will be contacted by the academic advisor, EDHE 105 instructor, and possibly others. These campus professionals will recommend the student start using the Writing Center. However, campus professionals can only encourage the student to utilize the resources that are available. Parents on the other hand, can require students to begin using the Writing Center through a variety of punitive measures. At the end of the day, it is up to an individual institution if they wish to include parents in their retention efforts. However, if it is believed that once some students get to college, they will cease communicating with their parents, and that the parents will comply with not being in the loop regarding their child's educational experience, then they may not be facing the reality of today's college student.

If parents are informed of important information regarding campus resources, dates, policies, and other reports, they can share this information with their students, thus helping the institution deliver important messages to students. We want to ensure our parents of freshmen are knowledgeable about University of Mississippi information and are thoughtful in how they offer advice from afar. Some of the information that I personally share with parents of freshmen is academic advising information. I inform parents where student advisor information is listed in their myOleMiss account. Furthermore, I advocate that parents encourage their students to contact the academic advisor for assistance. Some parents may want to contact the advisor directly, and we do allow that if the student has released academic information to the parent; however, my first piece of advice to parents is to let the student address his/her issue. It is helpful for parents to be able to remind their student where to find their advisor's contact information and to offer advice on how to interact with the advisor. This additional guidance can reduce the number of parents trying to work out their students' issues and assist students in learning how to handle their own issues while in college. The information that I share with parents is very general and can be found on the University's website. Others types of information I share with parents include: the University calendar, final exam schedule, campus resources, and special guidance based on where we are in the semester.

The University of Mississippi's freshman class includes more non-residents than Mississippi residents. These non-residents pay the same tuition and fees as residents, but are also charged an additional non-resident fee. For new freshmen in the 2016 cohort, the non-resident fee is $13,230 per year. I cannot tell you how many times over the years I have heard a non-resident parent say, "I'm paying a lot of money for my child to go to school there" or something similar. Usually this line is used when the parent wants something. It would be easy to respond, "I realize you pay a lot of money to send your child to school here, but college is expensive and you reminding me about the cost of attendance has no bearing on if I will be able to help address your issue." However, I let them throw out that line while they are explaining the problem their student is encountering. From a pure retention perspective, it does not matter if a student is receiving a full academic scholarship, is full Pell eligible, or paying the entire cost out-of-pocket. We are going to help all students regardless of their ability to pay. However, it is important to understand that parents who control the financial component of a student's college experience need to be treated as an ally. By keeping these parents informed and on our side of the retention battle, they are more likely to continue paying for their child to attend the University. Again, we are not going to do anything different based on how much someone is paying, but if you make parents feel involved and connected to their child's experience, they are more likely to provide financial support, thus contributing to the University's retention effort.

One line I say each year at the welcome of every orientation session goes something like this: "Parents, we see you as an ally. We want to keep you in the loop regarding important University information. We both have the same goal and that is for your freshman to have a great experience here at the University of Mississippi." I cannot overstate that last line. Both the institution and parents share the same goal. That goal is for each and every new freshman to have a great experience while successfully transitioning into a successful college student. Furthermore, making the social, academic, and personal adjustment during the first year benefits the student, parents, and the institution. We see a wide variety of parent interaction, especially during a new freshman's first semester. Some inquiries make us roll our eyes, while others are legitimate concerns that could lead to potential retention issues. For example, if a mom from California contacts me about her freshman having trouble finding his niche, being homesick, and thinking about leaving the University, then it is in my best interest to attempt to get the student connected ASAP. Another concern I hear frequently from parents usually happens after the student has done poorly on their first big test, paper, or other graded work. Parents contact me and assert that their child has never received such a low grade and is not only struggling in a specific course, but also is questioning if our University is a good fit. Although I am confident the student has previously heard about the various campus academic resources that could help, this parent interaction allows me to inform them about how to best help their child. At the end of the day, we want the student to earn a good grade and have a good experience, but also demonstrate to parents that we are committed to helping students be successful. While such an interaction with parents can have an immediate benefit of helping their student do better in the course, it may also be a factor in parents informing prospective students and their parents about how much the University of Mississippi cares about their students. Although there have been some cases in which I would rather have not promoted the involvement of parents, I can personally say that the vast majority of parent interaction has been beneficial to all parties involved.

START THE PARENT PARTNERSHIP EARLY AND REMAIN CONSISTENT

Do most prospective new freshmen take college visits alone? Of course not. Many come with an adult authority figure who can provide guidance. In my experience these adult authority figures are usually parents. Our institution does a good job during the recruitment of new students to make both the students and the parents feel like they are part of the college experience. During campus tours, presentations, recruiting fairs, and other student recruitment related activities, the admissions staff and other members of the campus community do their best to talk directly with the students, while making sure parents are included in the conversation. We realize that for many prospective students, their parents will play a significant role in where they attend college. Therefore, selling the parent on the institution's support and resources is very important in student recruitment. With that said, once you convince parents that your institution is the best fit for their child, it is important that you follow through with promises made during recruitment. In our case, we promise to keep parents in the loop regarding their child's college experience and welcome them to contact University staff members should they have any questions or concerns during the first year.

After the recruitment phase and once students have selected our institution, we began forming partnerships with parents as early as summer orientation. I speak at the morning welcome of each session. My brief talk focuses on how we view parents as partners, services of the Center for Student Success and First-Year Experience (CSSFYE), and information about EDHE 105. I wrap up the five-minute welcome by encouraging

Question:

Why is it important for an institution to view parents as partners?

new freshmen and parents to contact the CSSFYE if they have questions regarding anything related to freshman year. Contact is welcome while they are on campus for orientation, during the remainder of summer before the semester begins, and, especially, during the fall and spring semester when retention issues may arise. At the end of the first day of each orientation session, all student affairs departments attend a dessert reception for parents. This event allows parents to get to know a campus professional from each student affairs department (e.g., Housing, Financial Aid, Campus Recreation, Career Center, etc.). Parents can ask specific questions, get a general overview of a department, or make a contact which they may need to call upon at a later date. The CSSFYE's

Dr. Kyle Ellis informing parents at orientation that he will be in regular communication with them during their child's freshman year.

associate director and I attend almost every parent reception. Parents are usually overloaded with information after a long day, so we remind them that we spoke at the welcome and can assist with "anything and everything freshman." At each reception numerous parents engage in conversations with us related to a variety of topics. For some of the topics, in which we have direct oversight (e.g., EDHE 105, freshman academic advising, and academic support), we can provide specific information. However, other inquiries may need to be referred to a more appropriate department, or we offer to seek the requested information and follow up with the parent the following day. Introducing ourselves to parents at orientation definitely helps us establish a partnership that can be mutually beneficial.

Holding true to my promise at orientation regarding monthly communication to parents, I send an e-mail to all parents at the end of the first week of the semester. The e-mail includes a range of information, much of which is very useful early in the semester. I begin by introducing myself and informing them why they are receiving the e-mail. Then I inform them about their students' academic advisors, how to find advisor information, and encourage them to have their freshmen contact the assigned academic advisor should the need arise. I then provide information and the University link to Parent Web IDs. If the student has given authorization, a parent may create a Parent Webbed. This tool allows parents to log on to our myOleMiss portal and access some of their student's information (e.g., grades, holds, financial information, etc.). Because courses can only be added through the second week of the semester, I provide parents with drop and add dates for individual courses. Furthermore, I remind parents that students are required to be enrolled in 12 hours to be considered full-time. Other important information I include relates to the Office of Financial Aid, Bursar, and Contractual Services. I include Contractual Services' information to advise them of the small time window students have to change their meal plan. All the information I provide is available to the public. I do not give specific details, but general information that is listed on the University's website. To close the e-mail, I encourage parents to contact me if they have questions or concerns and to "like/follow" our social media accounts. Surprisingly, the CSSFYE's social media accounts receive lots of new "likes" and "follows" after this initial e-mail is sent. Informing parents of University information and opening the lines of communication early in the semester have been beneficial in our student support and retention efforts.

Ways to communicate with parents

There are several ways an institution can communicate with parents. In my experience, all forms of communication are important, but some are more effective than others. I highlighted a few of these earlier in this section, but wanted to provide more details on the individual methods.

Recruiting Events: Before students officially become part of a freshman cohort, it is important to get to know their support system (e.g., parents, guardians, family members). The University's Office of Admissions organizes numerous recruiting events and individual visits throughout the year. During these opportunities to interact with prospective students and their guests, it is important to speak directly with the student about their future educational experience. However, it is equally important to talk with members of their support system. Institutional representatives can inform the prospective student's guests about campus resources, student expectations, and how parents can remain involved in the student's college education. Remember, the institution is not only selling to the student, they also are convincing the student's support system that their school is the best place for academic, social, and post-graduation success.

Freshman Orientation: At the University of Mississippi, freshman orientation occurs the summer before new students being their higher educational journey. From the institution's perspective, this engagement

Parents are encouraged to attend Orientation with their incoming freshman.

opportunity is more important than an Admissions' event, as these students are more likely to be a part of the official freshman cohort. Therefore, any parent with which we interact can assist with retention efforts. Furthermore, campus representatives should expect more specific questions regarding institutional resources and support services. This is a prime opportunity to make parents feel welcomed and a part of their student's educational experience. Our University allows numerous campus professionals to speak during orientation and even offers a special parent schedule, which differs slightly from the new students. During these information sessions, parents are educated on University resources, polices, and other useful information. Additionally, we encourage open conversation throughout the two-day orientation. From orientation sessions and meals, to the receptions and informal conversations, parents are encouraged to ask any questions that may relate to their child's education at the University of Mississippi.

Monthly e-mails: Since 2013 I have made it a practice to send parents a monthly e-mail. During my welcome address at freshman orientation I announce that I will keep parents in the loop via my monthly e-mails. I use e-mail addresses that were included on the student's admission application. These addresses are uploaded to our campus management system and listed on a student's profile. Using a quick online data collection command, a report containing all parent e-mail address can be obtained. Our office takes that process a few steps further. In order to ensure our list is as accurate as possible, we send letters to the home addresses of all invalid e-mails that are returned as non-deliverable. In the letter we include the information from the initial e-mail, and also inform recipients

University of Mississippi Center for Student Success & FYE

@OleMissCSSFYE

Like   Follow   Message   More

Home

About

Photos

Likes

Posts

Create a Page

Status   Photo / Video

Write something on this Page...

University of Mississippi Center for Student Success & FYE
November 11 at 8:05am ·

Congratulations to Dr. Vitter on his investiture as the 17th Chancellor of the University of Mississippi!!
https://t.co/qBdEssFNGY

Investing in our future: Inauguration of Jeffrey Vitter - The Daily Mississippian

"Dr. Vitter, do you accept this charge?" "Hell yeah. Damn right," Chancellor Jeffrey Vitter responded, a...

THEDMONLINE.COM/INVESTING-FUTU...

Like   Comment   Share

University of Mississippi Center for Student Success & FYE
November 4 at 8:30am ·

Planning to be in town for Thanksgiving? Come out to join Campus Recreation in the 2016 Turkey Trot! https://t.co/190fRoTMYJ

Student Success &FYE (@OleMissCSSFYE) posted a photo on Twitter

Get the whole picture - and other photos from Student Success &FYE

PIC.TWITTER.COM/190FROTMYJ | BY STUDENT SUCCE

Like   Comment   Share

2

Write a comment...

Education

Search for posts on this Page

1,361 people like this

Invite friends to like this Page

ABOUT

P.O. Box 1848-350 Martindale 38677   Sav...

+86 2 915 5970

Ask for University of Mississippi Center for Student Success & FYE's hours

http://www.cssfye.olemiss.edu/

PHOTOS

VISITOR POSTS

Chat (29)

that their e-mail address was bounced back to us. We then provide a staff member's e-mail address in which the person with the non-deliverable address can send us a new e-mail so we may update their information. We receive numerous responses after the first e-mail, thus ensuring our contact attempts are reaching as many people as possible.

My e-mails give general University information (e.g., important dates, policies, campus resources, how to find useful information, etc.), while advocating for parents to encourage their freshmen to try to addresses their own issues. However, I also offer the opportunity for parents to contact me directly for assistance. Although most of the parental feedback I receive comes via e-mail, I do receive a fair amount of phone calls. While on the phone with parents, I do my best to provide a resolution to their issue. However, it is not uncommon for me to refer the parent to a colleague on campus for issues outside of my area of oversight. In my opinion, a referral to a specific person on campus is a major strength of our student support efforts. I will never tell a parent to call a 1-800 number, or check with fill in the blank department. I provide the parents with a specific point-of-contact regarding the issue. Based on feedback from both parents and even colleagues from other large institutions, my approach is a rare, but welcomed approach to student success. According to others, it is common practice for large institutions to pass parents off to a call center or another department which may or may not be able to help, or to simply tell the parent the student will have to find a way to resolve the issue. Regardless if a parent contacts an institutional representative via e-mail or phone, it is important to provide them with the appropriate information (as FERPA allows) and keep them engaged in the student's educational journey.

Social Media: Institutions of higher learning know that almost all of their students are active on social media. However, it is equally important to understand that parents also are active on various social media

outlets. Almost all University of Mississippi departments and programs have social media accounts. These accounts are vital mediums in our communication efforts. Unfortunately, just having a social media account is not enough. One must be active on those platforms. On all of my parent e-mails, I encourage them to like/follow the Center for Student Success and First-Year Experience's social media accounts. We have a dedicated staff member who oversees our accounts. This person has a directive to take recommendations as to what to post, like, share, follow, etc., but also responds to communication that occurs on our social media outlets. Although the Center for Student Success and First-Year Experience's social media accounts post information for student consumption, we encourage parents to follow/like us so they are in the loop regarding important information that can help their student be successful at the University.

Standard Mail: As previously mentioned in the e-mail section, I send a letter to the home address for all invalid parent e-mail addresses that

Author's Advice:

The CSSFYE social media pages have almost as many parents liking/following as we do students.

are bounced back. Another example of a standard mail form of contact I use involves sending letters to the home addresses of freshmen who enrolled with us in the fall, but did not return for the spring semester. This letter is sent in mid-April and is addressed to the student. However, many of the students are not living at home while they are attending a new institution. From my experience, the parent will open the letter and inform the student of the content. Although we, typically, do not have a large number of students, who receive the letter, contact us about returning, we do have some each year who will reference the letter and their desire to return to the University. For those readers who work in the world of retention, we know that every student counts. Therefore, if my letter is only successful in encouraging five students to return, that is a tenth of a retention point, and considered well worth the effort.

Other departments on campus send standard mail as well. These pieces of communication can include: Mid-term and final grades - Registrar's Office, Bills - Bursar's Office, and financial information (e.g., scholarships, loans, etc.) - Office of Financial Aid. Although those specific examples do not come from me, I often get questions, as grades and financial issues are related to retention. For example, when mid-term grades are mailed home (students and parents can also view grades online), I include academic resources in my parent e-mail that month. Parents often see the grades, then contact me with specific questions. Additionally, when referencing financial information in my monthly e-mails, I always include Bursar and Financial Aid contact information. Timing my e-mailed information, with the standard mail that comes from other departments, has been beneficial. This model allows parents to receive the information, have conversations with their student, develop questions, then contact the appropriate department on campus. Increasing efficiency and effectiveness of our efforts is an ongoing process. Finding ways to keep parents informed, so they may serve as an ally in University retention efforts, should be a strategy that all institutions implement.

Parent Inclusion

Does your institution encourage parents of freshmen to be involved during the first year? If so, please think about the following components: Who provides information to parents of freshmen?:

_____

_____

_____

_____

Topics covered:

_____

_____

_____

_____

How is this interaction beneficial to retention efforts?:

_____

_____

_____

_____

Brainstorm ways to partner with parents of freshmen during the first year.

_____

_____

_____

_____

_____

Example of Parent Communication Success

The e-mail chain below is a real example of how partnering with parents can help retention efforts. This student did very well academically, but we were on the verge of losing her due to not making a significant connection. I am confident this student would have transferred to a school closer to home had her mother not reached out to me, and we were able to intervene. Additionally, I spoke with her mother on the phone and the student did benefit from meeting with others who are referenced in the email chain. Names and identifying information has been retracted.

Emails are listed in the order which they occurred.

On Mar 25, 201X, at 10:06 AM, [Mother's name] wrote:

Hi Kyle,

My daughter, [Daughter's name], is struggling with her personal connections at Ole Miss. We met you at freshman orientation and I am impressed with your e-mail connections to parents. It's because of my deep concern for [Daughter's name] emotional wellness that I'm writing you.

She is excelling in academics, but has said she is sad and doesn't fit in at school. She has begun looking at other [Academic] programs and thinks she may find friends at another school.

I would like your team to help in connecting and researching the root causes in understanding [Daughter's name] situation. I want her to be successful socially and academically in order for her to be happy.

Thanks for your reply and please call as well.

All my best,

[Mother's Name]

On Mar 25, 201X, at 4:49 PM, Kyle Ellis wrote:

Hi [Mother's name],

I'm sorry to hear that [Daughter's name] is having trouble finding her niche socially. Do you know if she attended the [Specific geographic location] Freshman Meet and Greet during the second week of school? We invited all new freshmen from various regions early in the semester as a way to help them connect with some other new freshmen from their area of the country. We have about 150 freshmen from [List of states invited to the specific meet and greet].

Unfortunately, the University is closed today so it will be Monday before I am able to proceed, but I do have three ideas for people who may be able to help her get connected:

1. [Campus professional in the Dean of Students Office]. [Professional's name] is the [Professional's title]. She oversees [Professional's job responsibilities]. She has been successful in meeting with students and helping them get connected.

2. [Assistant Dean in the daughter's academic school]. [Assistant Dean's name] is the [Assistant Dean's title]. [Assistant Dean's name] is very nice and can possibly help her get connected within the [Academic school] and/or with other like-minded girls.

3. [Freshman from the prior year]. [Freshman from prior year's name] is from [State close to this student] and was a freshman last year. I received an email from [Freshman from prior year's name] mother that was similar to yours. After sharing some ideas with her mom and getting [Freshman from prior year's name] connected to other campus professionals, not only did she stay at UM, she has thrived. She started the [University club] participates in University events, and works as a [On campus job]. I'm confident [Freshman from prior year's name] can relate to how [Daughter's name] may be feeling, and can offer good advice.

Additionally, I will be happy to meet with [Daughter's name] if you believe it will be beneficial. If you give me the "go ahead" I will begin reaching out to the people listed above on Monday. Take care.

Kyle

Sent from my iPad

-----Original Message-----
From: [Mother's name]
Sent: Saturday, March 26, 201X 8:06 AM
To: Kyle Ellis
Subject: Re: [Daughter's name]

Hi Kyle,

Those all seem like great steps! I will talk with [Daughter's name] today and see if we can get her some connections Monday.

Happy Easter and many thanks!

Looking forward to our next steps.

Yours,

[Mother's Name]

-------- Original Message --------
Subject: RE: [Daughter's name]
From: Kyle Ellis
Date: Mon, March 28, 201X 10:05 am
To: [Mother's name]

Hi [Mother's name],

I'm touching base to see if you spoke to [Daughter's name] and would like for me to proceed with bringing other campus colleagues into the loop.

Kyle Ellis, Ph.D.
Director
Center for Student Success & First-Year Experience
The University of Mississippi

Phone call between Kyle and the mother to discuss how to proceed.
Monday, March 28, 201X

From: [Mother's name]
Sent: Wednesday, April 27, 201X 10:03 AM
To: Kyle Ellis
Subject: RE: [Daughter's name]

Hi Kyle,

[Daughter's name] is going to continue at Ole Miss. She has spoken with [Assistant Dean in the daughter's academic school] and will be taking classes in June to align her work with the [Academic major] she was accepted to.

Right now, she is trying to find housing for June. Do any of the dorms stay open for June programs?

Thank you for your continued guidance!

All my best,

[Mother's name]

INITIATIVE 8
SUPPORT FROM THE OFFICE OF FINANCIAL AID

The importance of having the Office of Financial Aid involved in retention efforts cannot be overstated. Each year the University of Mississippi loses numerous freshmen who cite financial concerns as their primary reason for not returning for a second year. The U.S. Census Bureau's American Community Survey (2008)1 ranked Mississippi 50th in the nation in median household income ($37,790). Many Mississippi freshmen begin at the University only to later realize they could save a lot of money by living at home and attending community college. Another important risk factor to note is the University's freshman class consists of more than 50% non-residents. Some of these students are financially at-risk to not persist, as they pay significantly more than Mississippi residents. These financial risk factors become a reality for front-line retention personnel every semester. Using our online retention tracking system, we know that the top two reasons 2014 freshmen cited for their departure were (number of cases): 1: Distance from home (110) and 2: Monetary reasons (108).

Top two reasons for freshman departure: 1: Distance from home and 2: Monetary reasons

The cost of higher education is going to continue to increase. Therefore, at an institution like the University of Mississippi, where resident students may come from lower socioeconomic families or a significant number of freshmen are non-residents and paying more in tuition, it is vital for the Office of Financial Aid to be an active partner in retention efforts.

Ways Financial Aid is Involved
in Retention Efforts

The Office of Financial Aid at the University of Mississippi is very engaged in the University's retention initiatives. Staff members in Financial Aid are aware that many freshmen leave the University due to financial concerns. The director is very supportive and has designated two specific staff members, the Associate Director and a Senior Financial Aid Advisor, to be the primary office liaisons who can work with all aspects of freshman retention. I can think of numerous examples where these two Financial Aid staff members have helped students who had financial concerns. When an academic advisor, EDHE 105 instructor, or another campus professional encounters freshmen who make it known that they may not return due to financial issues, they refer the student to the two specific Financial Aid staff members. These staff members can explore all possible financial options that may allow the student to return. If they are able to assist and the student had a financial hold, which prevented them from registering for the upcoming semester, the Financial Aid staff member completes the circle by informing students' academic advisor that they are now able to register for courses. Additionally, these campus professionals have access to the University's online retention tool so they can add notes about individual students. This is very useful to everyone on campus who is involved in retention efforts. If Financial Aid has already explored all possible financial options for a student and has documented doing so in the tool, then there is no point for an academic advisor, housing staff member, etc. to continue contacting the student about returning to the University. Having specific people in Financial

Aid who understand and care about student persistence has been very beneficial in our retention efforts.

One way the Office of Financial Aid is being more proactive in their involvement with retention is to do more financial education with students and families before the student officially enrolls at the University. This education occurs during campus visits, admissions' recruiting events, and online/printed literature. There is nothing more frustrating than speaking with a student or parent who states the student had a great experience at the University, but it is too expensive to continue their education at Ole Miss. I want to say, "Did you not understand the cost to attend the University before officially becoming part of our freshman cohort?" The cost of attendance is public information and students and parents are frequently made aware of how much it costs to attend the University. So to hear the experience was great and a student's grades are good, yet he/she is leaving because it "costs too much," can be difficult for someone like me who thinks about retention on a daily basis.

Undergraduate Student Enrolled Full-time	
Expense	Undergraduate
Tuition	$7,344.00
Capital Improvements Fee	$100.00
Housing	$5,730.00
Food	$4,398.00
Books/Supplies	$1,200.00
Personal/Travel	$4,600.00
Total for Residents	$23,372.00
Additional Fee for Nonresidents	$13,230.00
Total for Nonresidents	$36,602.00

2015-16 Cost of Attendance

In 2015 the Director of Financial Aid began to ask parents about their plan to pay for college during a parent-only orientation session. The director distributed handouts featuring the cost of attendance and asked parents to write out their financial plan. We are hopeful this was an eye-opening experience for some parents. As much as we do not want to see parents and students attend summer orientation, then not enroll for the fall, if they are forced to think about how much it costs to attend the University then make an informed decision not to attend based on costs, then I believe we have done both the family and the University a service. Although I am unaware of any families who chose not to enroll after factoring their ability to pay, we continue to see some freshmen, who say they enjoyed their time, but later leave for community colleges in-state or near their home, citing financial issues. When I have heard this reason given since we included the new financial aid planning meeting, I want to ask, "Did you not understand the material presented during the financial aid session at summer orientation?" Anecdotally, the two staff members in Financial Aid who directly assist with retention have shared some funny, yet frustrating examples from parents whose freshmen attended the University, but then left after their first year. One of the more common responses parents give when they are questioned about their knowledge of the cost of attendance and their financial plan goes something like this: "Student's name had his/her heart set on going to Ole Miss. Even though I knew it was expensive, I didn't have it in me to tell him/her that we could not afford it." In my opinion that is even worse than telling the student "no" upfront, or at least after orientation. Now the student enjoyed his/her experience, and in most cases had good grades, but is forced to start over at a school closer to home due to financial reasons. I am hopeful the Office of Financial Aid will continue to improve their financial education early in the process so students and families fully understand what it costs to attend the University and can make informed decisions before becoming official members of our freshman cohort.

Financial Aid on the Retention Advisory Board

The University of Mississippi's Retention Advisory Board has two members from the Office of Financial Aid. The Board is fortunate that both the Director and Associate Director of Financial Aid are willing to devote their time to retention efforts. As previously mentioned in Initiative 3, the Retention Advisory Board oversees all aspects of freshman retention. Therefore, even though Financial Aid board members can offer valuable insight and support regarding financial-related retention issues, they also are involved in discussions that fall outside their purview. The University's Retention Advisory Board, which consists of members, such as the two from Financial Aid, who understand our retention culture and are willing to support our efforts, is one of the primary factors that makes the University's retention efforts successful.

There are several examples of the ways Financial Aid has directly contributed to the work of the Retention Advisory Board. When the Board functioned as a steering committee and retention work was performed by committee members, the Financial Aid representative began a process of having financial aid advisors contact freshmen who had not registered and had a financial hold due to owing the University money. Since its inception, this system has improved and is now very efficient. Rather than being reactive after priority registration has occurred, Financial Aid Advisors begin reviewing accounts of freshmen who have large balances early in the semester. By contacting these students early, and in some cases working with their parents, advisors can release students' financial holds before priority registration, which allows them to select courses as soon as their windows open. Of course, there are still reactive efforts when lists of no-schedule freshmen are generated after all registration windows have opened. The Financial Aid board members provide the group with regular updates regarding their efforts to help no-schedule freshmen with financial barriers get their holds resolved.

The members from Financial Aid have been important allies when the Retention Advisory Board has discussed University policies that have financial implications. For example, the Board has attempted to get the University to offer formalized payment plans which students may opt to utilize. The Board believed that allowing students and parents to sign up for payment plans would decrease the amount of freshmen who owe thousands of dollars as the semester is coming to a close. Personally, I would support all freshmen being required to participate in a payment plan if they were unable to pay the full tuition up front or did not have a financial aid package that would cover the costs. As previously stated, there is nothing more frustrating than students who enjoy their experience at the University, who then leave citing financial concerns, because they or their parents never planned for how they would pay for college. Throughout the payment plan process, Financial Aid staff provided the Board with insight, examples from other institutions, and attended the proposal meeting with the Bursar's Office. Unfortunately, the Bursar's Office was not in favor of creating and marketing payment plans, but it was important to get the conversation started with all necessary parties. Following this unsuccessful venture, the Director of Financial Aid agreed to increase their educational efforts to both prospective students and their parents. The Financial Aid members on the Retention Advisory Board are greatly appreciated for their direct and indirect contributions to the University's retention initiatives.

Freshman Retention Funds

The University realizes that some freshmen may fall on hard times financially, or that their financial plan (if they had one) did not cover fully all costs associated with attending the University of Mississippi. Therefore, in 2008 the Retention Advisory Board submitted a proposal to the Provost's Office for funding dedicated to freshman retention. The provost approved and allocated funds to be used at the discretion of Financial Aid. Financial Aid wanted to make a significant impact, so they decided to award smaller amounts to students in good standing who could pay an equal amount of their remaining balance. For example, if a freshman owed $2,000 and had good grades, Financial Aid would award $1,000 of one-time retention money if the student was able to pay the remaining $1,000. Once the student made the payment, Financial Aid would notify the Bursar's Office and the financial hold would be removed from the student's account. The retention funds were limited so Financial Aid had to be strategic in how they allocated the funds. With only a set amount of one-time money to use, it would not be wise to help a student who owed a large sum such as $10,000. Helping these types of students would (a) quickly deplete the funds; (b) not be a good investment, as the student could potentially be in the same scenario the following semester; and (c) put them at a disadvantage, as many students would not be able to come up with $5,000 out-of-pocket. Additionally, Financial Aid would review grades in order to make an informed decision on their investment. It would not be wise to give a student with a 1.0 GPA, funding as he/she may not return the following semester. Good investments are freshmen with high GPAs, low balances, and reasonable explanations of why the one-time funding will help them make it to the next semester. When students and parents accept the funding, it is explained to them that this funding is one-time and the family must have a plan on how they will be able to cover the full amount owed during future semesters.

Retention funds are utilized during both fall and spring semesters. However, spring retention funds have more priority, as they impact the fall-to-fall retention rate (i.e., the rate that counts in official measurements). Although the money may be awarded during the end of the spring semester or summer, it is not disbursed until the fall semester, thus ensuring the student returns to campus. Additionally, when Financial Aid is considering using some of the funds for freshmen in the spring, they can see if the student was able to pay for the fall semester. This supports my earlier premise in that Financial Aid wants to safeguard their investment by awarding the funding to freshmen who are most likely to persist. If students and their parents are having trouble paying for the first fall semester of college, and do not have a reasonable explanation as to how they will be able to pay for future semesters, then Financial Aid would consider that information when making funding decisions. However, some funding is awarded in the fall semester that is utilized to help freshmen persist from fall to spring. Although there is not as much time in between the fall and spring semester when compared to spring to fall, Financial Aid is able to view needy students' fall grades and have conversations with them and/or their parents. In the future, University leadership is considering a new retention funding model where the amount awarded is based on final grades. The maximum amount is to be determined. This model may cause a decrease in the number of students who are able to be helped. However, more financial investment in "better" students may yield higher persistence rates in the future. Numerous freshmen have benefited thanks to the University's retention funds.

Assistance from the Bursar

The Bursar's Office has been a friend to the Retention Advisory Board in recent years. After priority registration has ended, the largest number of freshmen who have yet to register have holds related to the Bursar's Office. In 2011 the provost reviewed a list of all freshmen who had not registered for the upcoming semester and owed money. He found the threshold to be $400. This amount is where a significant number of freshmen could be helped; while the amount was not insurmountable, it was believed that most students would be able to pay it off. The provost asked the Bursar's Office to temporarily remove the holds for all freshmen who owed $400 or less. The Bursar's Office agreed and the holds were removed for a three-week window so these freshmen and others who could get their balance to $400 or less could register for the upcoming semester. There were two primary considerations for the Bursar's Office when they agreed upon the timeline for hold removal. They wanted the holds to be removed after the 15th of the month, as holds are set on the 15th of every month. Therefore, if they lifted the holds before the 15th they would have had to go back and remove them again. The Bursar's Office was adamant about the holds going back on by the Tuesday of finals week. This ensured that final grades had not been recorded on transcripts. Students are not allowed to receive a transcript if they owe the University money. The University has maintained the temporary financial hold removal for freshmen owing $400 or less each semester since the provost originally advocated for this initiative. The fall dates are November 16-18 through the Tuesday of finals week in December. Thanksgiving Break week falls in this time span, so not much face-to-face support is accessible while the students have already gone home for the holiday. The spring dates are April 16-18 through the Tuesday of finals week in May. During the fall 2015 temporary hold removal period, there were 80 freshmen who qualified for this opportunity. In spring 2016, there were 83 freshmen who fell under the original $400 or less threshold.

Notifying the freshmen who are afforded the opportunity of having their financial hold temporarily removed is a team effort. The Center for Student Success and First-Year Experience (CSSFYE) assistant director-retention is the primary person who compiles the list of no-schedule freshmen who owe $400 or less. She then sends the Bursar's Office the list of freshmen who qualify. Once the holds have been removed, she e-mails all freshmen on the list. The e-mail explains why the hold is being temporarily removed, the time-frame in which it will be reactivated, and the importance of registering for classes as soon as possible. Following that notification, she shares lists with academic advisors, dean's offices, first-year experience instructors, and special cohort owners. Everyone understands time is of the essence so it is extremely important that professionals from across campus are sending the message to register for classes immediately before the hold is reactivated.

Furthermore, the Bursar's Office has been agreeable to temporarily remove the hold for freshmen who can get their balance down to $400 or less during the three-week window. The aforementioned campus professionals are aware of this and work with other no-schedule freshmen to get the balance down so they, too, can take advantage of this opportunity. Additionally, the CSSFYE Assistant Director-Retention shares a list of freshmen who owe between $401-$1,000 and who have not registered for the upcoming semester with academic advisors. The advisors work with those freshmen who can register immediately, but also inform those with reasonable balances about the opportunity to register if they can get their balance down during the temporary hold removal period. Financial Aid advisors also are very active during this time period in helping students get balances down so they may register. Whether it is encouraging freshmen to pay some money to get under the threshold, exploring other financial opportunities to support the students, or offering one-time retention funds, the Financial Aid staff plays a vital role in freshmen getting registered and removed from the no-schedule list.

The Office of Financial Aid can have a tremendous impact on an institution's retention rate.

Both the Office of Financial Aid and the Bursar's Office need to be included in retention efforts. From assisting students in understanding the cost of attendance to working with families on a case-by-case basis, Financial Aid can have a tremendous impact on an institution's retention rate. The University of Mississippi is fortunate that the Bursar's Office is willing to assist in our efforts. Their generous opportunity for select freshmen allows students to bypass a barrier and get registered. We are aware that students who register earlier create a more preferable schedule and persist at higher rates when compared to their peers who register at later dates. I strongly encourage anyone who works with retention to include offices that oversee financial aspects, as professionals in these areas make great partners.

The Financial Aid Office and Office of the Bursar are located in the Martindale Student Services Center.

Support from the Office of Financial Aid

Is the Office of Financial Aid currently involved in your retention efforts? If so, please think about the following components:

Who are the direct retention-related points of contact in the Financial Aid office?:

_____

_____

_____

_____

How does their involvement benefit freshman retention?:

_____

_____

_____

_____

Brainstorm ways to further include the Office of Financial Aid in retention efforts.

_____

_____

_____

_____

_____

_____

_____

Interview

Laura Diven-Brown
Director of the Office of Financial Aid

Describe your role in the University's retention efforts.

As the Director of Financial Aid, I oversee efforts to help students who are at risk of dropping out due to financial problems. My office's proactive involvement began in 2008 when we were given a small pool of funds, and charged with figuring out how to distribute them to increase retention rates. So we took a look at those students with billing holds that were preventing them from registering for the upcoming semester. The goal was to determine whether a one-time "leg up" would help them stay in school.

I will say that it's not as easy as it sounds to identify those students who are having financial difficulties. You can't just run a report and find them all. Of course, the results of the FAFSA (Free Application for Federal Student Aid) are useful for reviewing which students demonstrate financial need by the federal definition, and we can check Bursar balances to see who owes the school money. But student/parent behaviors and attitudes are also important influences.

For example, there are students that are successfully managing their money and minimizing debt by being frugal (such as choosing less expensive residence halls and meal plans, and riding the bus versus keeping a car on campus). They may also be working part-time. It is also possible that relatives outside their primary household are contributing to college costs. On the other hand, a student with a higher calculated EFC (Expected Family Contribution) may have a FAFSA that does not reflect the fact that a parent recently lost his or her job, or is dealing with high medical bills. So that is why our very first efforts to help freshmen began with phone calls. I was convinced that the only way we were going to understand each student's situation was to talk to them – or their parents.

And sure enough, as we did that, we found that many students and their families with outstanding bills were just procrastinating payment, and were not a risk at all – and others were struggling with hidden issues like health problems and loss of income. Some students were overwhelmed or unsure about financial aid requirements, and just needed support and instruction for completing the application processes. In fact, we have helped hundreds of students by merely connecting them to standard financing options like Federal Work-Study and Direct Loans. We also were able to re-evaluate eligibility for need-based aid for students who were experiencing significant, documented financial hardships.

Some students truly did benefit from small amounts of need-based institutional assistance to get them on the right track at this critical point in their college experience. But we learned over time to emphasize cost-sharing, versus hand-outs – and start conversations about budgeting. And then there were cases when it wasn't really about having enough money for college at all – the students were not coming back for other reasons – personal reasons, or things that they had not discussed with anyone on campus. Sometimes they could be referred to other offices that could address those needs. But we would not have known if we hadn't asked.

It is important to add that we must consider grades in all this. Realistically, we cannot provide special funding to a student who is not performing well academically and is not on track to graduate. We don't want to fix the retention problem on a short-term basis only. But there are many reasons why a GPA may be low, and our advisors attempt to find out if there are any extenuating circumstances that may have disadvantaged the student.

At Ole Miss, similar to other institutions, our students have higher "direct" costs in the first year. I'm referring to the charges that the college directly bills them (as opposed to "indirect" costs of attendance like personal and travel expenses). Freshmen are required to live on campus, so in addition to tuition and books, they have upfront housing and meal charges to cover. Since their bills are higher as a result, we often see numerous unpaid balances when the time comes around to register for the next semester. If we can intervene early, then we may be able to help them complete their first year of college, knowing that future years will allow them more choices with living arrangements.

Hopefully we are also teaching them to develop viable financial plans for the subsequent school years. It is essential to plan ahead – as a family. We are aware that most parents are the ones handling the finances, but Financial Aid urges them to include their sons and daughters in the process so the students learn how, too.

In your opinion, what are some of the most effective retention strategies at the University?

I have always said that the proactive calling campaigns we have, which now involve many offices across campus – from academic advisors to Student Services departments – are effective in and of themselves, even if we can't do much more than listen to their concerns. The students and families appreciate that the University cares enough to reach out to them. So the time we invest in this work is well-spent, and shows good faith.

I also think we have successfully developed programming for students who need support when they first come to Ole Miss. The transition to college can be daunting for some of them. That has been a bigger need these days - recent generations seem to be more dependent on their parents, so we are returning to "in loco parentis". Some examples include the EDHE 105 - First Year Experience Course, which helps them bond to Ole Miss and get to know fellow freshmen in a class setting that allows discussion and reflection. FASTrack is another opportunity for students to voluntarily participate in a cohort experience that involves targeted advising and smaller classes. We also have Luckyday Success and the Ole Miss Women's Council, who offer scholarship programs with mentoring components. And our "first alert" monitoring has become more comprehensive – where we try to identify students who are not engaged, and are in danger of not being retained – by looking for whether they have had multiple absences, failed to scan their ID card for meals, etc.

Since you became involved in the University's retention efforts, describe some changes you have observed.

I have definitely noticed that our campus efforts are more coordinated, and people are not working in silos anymore. Our interdisciplinary retention committee meets regularly, which allows us to compare notes on a frequent basis. Institutional Research tracks the retention numbers during registration periods – distributing daily reports to all participating internal departments so we can review ongoing progress and fluctuations, and compare the numbers to previous years, side-by-side. We all stay alert and aware.

In addition, my office was an early advocate for creating a freshman retention database that would keep consolidated case notes about individual students. Multiple offices use this tool, which was created by in-house IT staff. So we have a lot more information at our fingertips now, and are not stepping on each other's toes by having everyone contact the students at the same time. We don't want to harass – we want to help.

Where do you see retention efforts going in the short term? Long term?

In the short-term, I think we have to fine-tune our efforts, but also find ways to reach out to families before they move their freshmen into the dorms for that first semester. I cannot stress enough that they need to be informed about college costs in advance, and have a financial plan in place for paying for everything. It is heartbreaking to see students who love their school, and are doing well grade-wise, but cannot afford it and have to leave. Unfortunately, there is not enough scholarship and grant funding to go around.

Part of that education will involve helping families think along the lines of making payments in manageable increments. On that front, Ole Miss will be researching the best approach for an institutional payment plan.

Financial problems are definitely on the list of top reasons why students don't return, but of course we know that there are others – like school "fit" and social belonging, distance from home, etc. And, of course, there are academic challenges. At Ole Miss, for example, our admission standards reflect the state of Mississippi's emphasis on access to higher education – particularly for state residents. So there are differences in how ready students are to take on the rigors of college-level work. Low grades can certainly impact future financial aid eligibility. And then the lack of financial resources increases student stress and poor performance, which becomes a vicious cycle.

We must continue to pursue services like tutoring help and study skills workshops. Some of our academic departments are responding by offering things like "Biology Boot Camp" in the summer before the freshman year, so students can try to catch up before launching into the regular school year. In addition, students should be encouraged to visit the Career Center for counseling, to ensure that their chosen degree program is a realistic match to their interests and abilities. This will also help them determine what kind of salary they can expect upon graduation – which is especially important for loan borrowers, who may not be thinking about the future and having enough money to pay off their debt.

In the long term, I believe that schools need to pursue predictive modeling that can help us to examine our own unique student populations. We have to be careful not to label students, but we should use data constructively to develop intervention strategies.

I also think that we must expand our efforts to look beyond the freshman year, to help students get to graduation. I would like to see an increase in funding for 4-year, need-based scholarship awards that can set students up for success over the course of their undergraduate program.

What advice would you give other institutions regarding their retention efforts?

Institutions should have the commitment of upper administration for their retention strategies. It is also a best practice to determine who takes the lead in coordinating efforts, and where this function should be housed. Many schools have Enrollment Management units, or student success offices, for this purpose.

Retention goals should be established that are realistic, yet challenge the institution to do more for the students. And without question, resources must be made available for campus initiatives –whether for retention micro-grants, or personnel for support programs. Schools demonstrate that they make retention a priority by funding these efforts. Financially, it is a smart decision. As they say, it costs more to recruit a new student than retain a current student - so it's certainly in the university's best interests. And to the student who is able to overcome obstacles and get a college degree, it is life-changing.

INITIATIVE 9
PARTNERING WITH HOUSING

The Department of Student Housing at the University of Mississippi plays an important role in freshman retention. New freshmen at the University are required to live on campus. Therefore, professional and student staff members have a unique opportunity to interact, educate, and support all new students living in residence halls. Furthermore, unlike learning and engagement opportunities in the classroom, Housing staff members have access to these students 24 hours a day, seven days a week during the semester. Staff members in the Housing Department not only provide proactive support to assist with freshman retention, they can also be reactive when the need arises. The Retention Advisory Board includes an administrator from Housing. This person is very engaged in all aspects of retention, but specifically supports various ways Housing can positively impact our retention rate. A different administrator also is involved in retention efforts, as she welcomes campus professionals to contact her with any retention-related housing issue. Additionally, the Director of Housing is very supportive of the University's retention efforts. I highly recommend including the Housing Department in an institution's retention plan.

Benefits of Including Housing

There are numerous ways staff members from the Housing Department can make contributions to retention efforts. Anyone who works with college students, especially freshmen, understands that most new students will have transition issues. For some, issues can be minor and easily overcome. For others, issues may escalate and the new student leaves the institution due to the inability to make a smooth transition from high school to college. These transition issues are examples of how Housing staff members can be both proactive and reactive in helping new students adapt to college life. Other than the classroom, new freshmen living on campus will spend a significant amount of time in their residence halls. With these students living on campus, Housing staff members can plan activities for the students, offer educational opportunities outside of the classroom, and provide students with individualized guidance should an issue arise. Most of the Housing staff that interacts directly with freshmen are undergraduate or graduate students who are employed by the Housing Department. These students go through many hours of training so they can address new freshman issues that may come up during the first year.

Each semester we lose new freshmen for a variety of issues that are not related to financial, health, or academic reasons. However, I can imagine we would lose a significant amount more if not for the good work by Housing staff members who address potential retention-related problems before they become reasons for students to leave the University. With over half the freshman class being non-residents, it is not uncommon for me to hear from students (and their parents) who are homesick. When these freshmen are brought to my attention, one of the first people I bring into the loop is an administrator from Housing. This person notifies the Community Assistant or the Graduate Hall Director who can contact the student. Once contact is made, the Housing staff member can offer guidance and help the new student get connected.

Housing staff members also are valuable in addressing roommate conflicts. On rare occasions I have heard from parents who tell me their freshman is leaving the University due to the student not getting along with a roommate. Housing has a system in place to address roommate conflicts. However, issues between roommates are not always able to be resolved. In these cases, a Housing administrator has allowed roommate swaps outside of the normal room change dates. One specific example that comes to mind is when a mother of a non-resident freshman female called me crying. The mother stated that she and her husband were about to get in the car, drive to Oxford, and remove her daughter from the University. This was roughly two months into the semester, so the daughter was officially part of the freshman cohort. According to the mother, the daughter and her roommate had been having issues for some time. They tried to go through the standard roommate conflict process, but the issues could not be resolved. Apparently, something had happened recently and the daughter called her mother upset saying she wanted to withdraw from the University. Her Community Assistant said it was outside the roommate swap period so the two girls would have to remain in the same room. Rather than have the parents drive 12 hours and remove the student from school, I called several Housing administrators and explained the situation. A few hours later the daughter was able to move to a different residence hall and her parents did not make the drive to Oxford. Had no one known how unhappy the daughter was, her parents would have moved her out and we would have lost a freshman in the middle of the semester over an issue that could have been resolved. From a retention viewpoint, we want students to be satisfied with their housing situation. I appreciate Housing's work and support in addressing potential issues that may result in a student leaving the University.

Housing staff members assisting new students during move-in

Housing Member on the Retention Advisory Board

As previously mentioned in Initiative 3, the University's Retention Advisory Board (RAB) is made up of institutional professionals from across campus. A representative from Housing was not included on the original Retention Steering Committee. However, when the group expanded, key areas that could have an impact on freshman retention were identified. The Department of Student Housing was one of the areas that we invited to send a representative. The new member from Housing was a welcome addition as he could make contributions directly on behalf of Student Housing, but could also offer input on other retention aspects.

One of the more successful initiatives that the Housing representative to the RAB oversees is the no-schedule follow-up by residence hall. Approximately one week before final exams the assistant director-retention in the Center for Student Success and First-Year Experience (CSSFYE) sends the RAB Housing representative a list of all freshman cohort members who have yet to register for the upcoming semester. It must be noted that the list does not include freshmen who have already informed us they plan to leave the University.

The list comprises those who have told us they are returning, but have a barrier or those whom we have been unable to contact. We strategically wait until close to the end of the semester so the list Housing receives is as small as possible. The list contains each student's on-campus housing assignment. The Housing professional who receives the list divides it by residence hall and sends individual reports to graduate hall directors and community assistants. These Housing staff members have at least one week to make contact with freshmen on their lists. In 2015 we attempted to train these front-line professionals on how to use our online retention tool so they could provide updates on each student. Unfortunately, having them input retention notes directly caused some minor discrepancies in our data. Therefore, it was decided the most efficient approach was for them to e-mail their notes to the CSSFYE assistant director-retention so she could insert them into the retention tool.

Question:
How can student housing be involved in your retention efforts?

These front-line staff members' interactions have been beneficial in reminding students, who have not registered and have a barrier, the importance of resolving their issue and getting a schedule for the upcoming semester; in addition, staff can gain access to information from freshmen whom other campus professionals have not been able to contact. At the conclusion of the "door knock campaign" we have information on almost the entire freshman cohort regarding their plans for the upcoming semester. Without the RAB Housing representative coordinating this valuable initiative, I am confident there would be freshmen, whose upcoming semester plans we would be unaware.

The RAB Housing representative also provides valuable input to issues that may or may not directly involve the Department of Student

Housing. With this person understanding the importance of freshman retention, it is not uncommon for him to interject various ways Housing can be involved in retention efforts, even if specific opportunities had no direct connection to Housing. For example, special cohorts are gaining popularity on campus. The cohorts connect students in a variety of ways. The Housing representative is always looking for ways to increase learning communities for students. Therefore, when a special cohort is under discussion, he is able to provide feedback as to whether a learning community for the cohort would be a good investment. The key to retaining freshmen is to make sure they are connected to the institution. If this can be accomplished solely through a special cohort, then I am fully supportive. However, if a special cohort combined with a learning community is the best approach, then that would be my choice as someone who places the highest importance on freshman retention. This RAB member also is active in educational opportunities within the residence halls. These programs may not be able to provide a direct correlation to freshman retention, but I believe the value they afford our freshmen has value in student persistence.

Completed in 2011, Burns Hall is a newer residence hall that houses freshmen.

Retention Data by Residence Hall

Since 2012, the University has collected and acted upon freshman retention data by residence hall. The University of Mississippi's enrollment has been growing at a tremendous rate over the last several years. This growth has led to new residence halls being built. Unfortunately, the newer facilities fill up first, leaving the most at-risk students to live among each other in older residence halls. In addition, the new residence halls that are nicer and have more amenities are more expensive, thus forcing lower socioeconomic freshmen (who we already know are at risk) to select older housing options. Obviously, forcing new freshmen who register for housing last or who come from lower socioeconomic families to live together is not the most opportune scenario for retaining these students.

By viewing retention rates for each residence hall, Housing Department administrators can determine the most appropriate use of their resources. At the University of Mississippi there was a male residence hall that traditionally filled up last, had a significant number of non-residents, and was one of the oldest housing facilities. It should be no surprise that this residence hall had the lowest retention rate for several years. The low retention data was very informative for upper-level Housing administrators, including the representative who serves on the Retention Advisory Board. They decided to place a full-time campus professional to oversee the residence hall, as opposed to a graduate hall director (i.e., a graduate student). This person could offer more educational opportunities, provide an adult presence in the hall, and potentially, have a better understanding of University resources and the value we place on freshman retention, thus have a vested interest in assisting each and every student within the hall. The ability to increase resources for this particular residence hall was proven to be successful, as after implementing this change that specific residence hall was no longer at the bottom of the retention rankings. I believe early efforts in tracking retention by residence hall have been beneficial, and have the potential to be even more dynamic, as we can now capture additional data through our new Tableau software. Making data-driven retention decisions is imperative in moving the retention needle. Now that we have the ability to not only look at retention by residence hall, but also view specific populations within the residence hall, our efforts can be more strategic in proactive retention planning.

Specific Initiatives in Which
Housing Contributes

As previously stated, the Department of Student Housing can be a valuable asset in an institution's freshman retention efforts. Some of Housing's initiatives at the University of Mississippi (e.g., no-schedule follow up, inserting notes in the online retention tool, etc.) have already been discussed in this initiative. However, other ways Housing assists in student persistence include staff members' involvement in our Freshman Attendance Based Initiative (FABI), offering programming in the residence halls, and addressing transition issues.

Freshman Attendance Based Initiative (FABI)

The Freshman Attendance-Based Initiative (FABI) program was launched in the Fall of 2001. This program targets freshman attendance in lower division courses. Using our web-based reporting tool, instructors report freshmen who have been absent three times or more during weeks 3-11 each semester. The Center for Student Success and First-Year Experience's assistant director-retention downloads this information weekly and disseminates reports across campus based on the established FABI communication model. Front line Housing staff members such as community assistants are the primary people involved in early intervention efforts. Community assistants are provided with a campus resource guide and have FABI training prior to the beginning of the fall semester. Community assistants visit the rooms of freshmen on the report. They have conversations that focus on the importance of going to class, campus resources, and other academic success-related topics. Additionally, this opportunity for interaction with a student who could be deemed as potentially at-risk due to poor class attendance, can open the door to other discussions that may impact the student's success and/or well-being. During the fall 2015 semester there were 5,473 students reported with at least three absences in a course. These were not unique students, as some students could have been reported multiple times for different classes. Additionally, not all of the students were freshmen, as some upperclassmen take 100- and 200-level courses. Regardless, if the students were reported for multiple classes or they were not freshmen, that number still contains a significant amount of freshmen in the cohort. By Housing taking an active role in attendance-intervention efforts, they are definitely making a difference in the academic and personal well- being of our freshmen.

Programming in Residence Halls

The University of Mississippi requires new freshmen to live on campus. This requirement allows Housing staff members to have frequent interaction with freshmen. One opportunity for interaction involving educational and social engagement is through programming in the residence halls. Housing staff members have the ability and some resources to schedule guest speakers, provide activities, and other programs that can educate their residents, as well as help them get connected to each other and the University. Programming can be implemented by floor, entire residence hall, and other ways residents can be grouped together.

Some examples of programs that have been offered in the past that the Center for Student Success and First-Year Experience (CSSFYE) have been involved with include study skills workshops, tips on preparing for successful meetings with academic advisors, and sessions on choosing a major. These sessions would all be classified as educational. The CSSFYE welcomed the opportunity to partner with Housing for these programs, as we understood the importance of the topics and how they can help our freshmen have a successful experience at the University. Other programs that I am aware of that have been offered in the residence halls include guest speakers from the Career Center, University Police Department, and the Dean of Students Office. Additionally, programs that are educational, but also social opportunities that have been offered include cooking demonstrations, group fitness, athletic activities, cultural presentations, and other examples in which students can increase their knowledge, well-being, and social network.

Addressing Transition Issues

Although there are several thousand faculty member, staff, and administrators on campus who care about students, few have the same opportunities that Housing staff members have regarding fostering individual relationships with our new freshmen. These relationships allow Housing staff members to get to know these students personally and to assist them if/when a transition issue arises. Based on past feedback from freshmen and their parents, some common

Freshmen at the University of Mississippi are required to live on campus during their first year.

transition issues experienced by new students include: adjusting to living with a roommate, homesickness, time management, understanding expectations of a college student, higher education academic demands, and being accountable for one's actions while experiencing the newfound freedom at the University. Any of the aforementioned transition issues could derail a new student and cause him/her to leave the institution, if the problem is not addressed. Housing can play a major role in both proactive and reactive outreach regarding these potential pitfalls. Through residence hall programming or individual meetings with community assistants or other members of the Department of Student Housing, these campus professionals have the opportunity to support and assist new freshmen to overcome any transition that may come their way.

Question:

How are relationships Housing staff members have with students beneficial to student persistence?

Partnering with Housing

Is the Department of Student Housing currently involved in your retention efforts? If so, please think about the following components:

Who are the direct retention-related points of contact in Housing?

_____

_____

_____

_____

_____

How does their involvement benefit freshman retention?

_____

_____

_____

_____

Brainstorm ways to further include the Department of Student Housing in retention efforts.

_____

_____

_____

_____

_____

_____

_____

INTERVIEW

Scott Oliver

Assistant Director of Student Housing for Residential Learning

Describe your role in the University's retention efforts.

I currently serve as the Assistant Director for Residential Learning and represent Student Housing on the University's Retention Advisory Board. My primary day to day role includes overseeing our residential curriculum model for student housing and helping to guide how we promote, connect, and integrate student learning into our residential environments. Part of this involves how students are connecting to the overall campus community and how residential environments can support collective campus efforts to help students be successful. Originally, I began working with the retention group a couple of years ago when I was asked to participate and evaluate the impact of residential environments on retention at the University. Specifically we were looking at how specialized programs like Living-Learning Communities contributed to retention of students on campus. We found that the overall residential experience was consistent with established research – that the residential experience contributes positively to retention of students in general. As part of the retention group, I serve as a liaison between the group and the work of the group and then work with our residential staff and help coordinate personal interaction with students.

In your opinion, what are some of the most effective retention strategies at the University?

In relation to my role with Student Housing – I think some of the most effective strategies are the ones that allow our team members within the living areas to make personal contact with students about their experiences and also to discuss and provide resources that contribute to student success. Personal connection and engagement is a primary strategy that we use to support retention. One of the considerations that is important to the way that we engage (and teach team members within housing to engage) with students living in our residence halls is that we work within the framework of a residential curriculum. This allows us to connect our educational priorities and also learning outcomes to the University experience. An example of such intentional engagement opportunities under this framework is that we partner with the Center for Student Success and First-Year Experience about our personal follow-up on FABI (Freshman Attendance-Based Initiative). Each Monday, during the first couple of weeks of the fall and spring semester - our graduate and professional housing team receives a list of students who were absent from classes in the previous week for their community. They coordinate with student peer leaders (Community Assistants) to make personal contact with students on their floors/areas. It is a way to make sure that our CAs are following up on our departmental educational priorities to help students become and be engaged scholars and responsible citizens. Other examples include supporting personal contact work and follow-up with students who have not yet registered for classes or address and follow-up personally with students who may have holds on their student accounts. An additional retention strategy within student housing and residential learning involves following up with students about personal issues or concerns that may be affecting their ability to study or engage with the University community – for example how they are connecting (or not

connecting) with their roommate or homesickness, involvement, and/
or community 'fit' – all things that could in various ways contribute
to a student's ability to connect and ultimately stay at the institution.

Since you became involved in the University's retention efforts, describe some changes you have observed.

Since becoming involved with the retention efforts on campus,
I think I have seen a greater understanding by staff at various levels
about how they contribute to the retention efforts of the University as a
whole. Retention is really an 'all-hands on deck' kind of effort, if efforts
are truly intended to be successful. This is the way that I talk about
retention with my residential living team members – they are helping
to ensure that students stay at the University through their personal
interactions and their personal support of students. We talk about the
role that our student staff members make in retention during training
and then follow-up with them in the form of numbers. I have also seen
a more intentional approach to how what we are doing in our normal
work can contribute to retention.

Where do you see retention efforts going in the short term? Long term?

In terms of UM, I would say in the short term – fall-to-fall first-
year retention will continue to be an important consideration of what
we do. Specifically within residential learning – because we have a current first-year live-on requirement and the overwhelming majority of
our on campus residential population is first and second year students.
That population is a major focus of our retention efforts. That being
said - having students stay at the University is important in general
because it is really the only way that the University is able to function.
In taking a bigger picture perspective, I think the overarching goal
is beyond just first-year retention – though that is mainly what the

retention group that I am a part of focuses on. Understanding how retention looks at all levels from the time students arrive until the time that they graduate with a degree in hand is the bigger picture. The ability to persist through the first year is important, but I think that is equally important in evaluating how we close any gaps that may exist between first-year retention and ultimate graduation rates. It's fine to start the race well but if you don't hit the finish line – you've not really completed the race. In terms of my role in residential learning, I think in both short term and long term planning, it helps me to attempt to look at how we are training and working with student staff (CAs, GAs, and the in-hall residence life team) to support not just our first and second year students in residential environments, but also how can we support – limited though they may be – those upper level students (juniors, seniors, and beyond) toward the ultimate goal of degree. Currently, we use our residential curriculum as a framework for how we approach such training, interactions, etc. Having an understanding of retention needs and efforts allows me to work with and support our student housing team to in turn best assist students. It also allows us to be intentional and strategic as we are planning or partnering with offices on campus to do things within the residence halls – how can the concept of retention be in the forefront of our planning and efforts and not an afterthought because it is being asked for as part of an assessment measure? It allows us to think forward and with purpose, being proactive instead of reactive. Ultimately, understanding why students stay and being able to be intentional and purposeful about how to best support them in their experience and eliminate obstacles to success contributes to the greater mission of the University.

What advice would you give other institutions regarding their retention efforts?

As I said previously, I think that retention is an 'all hands on deck' effort in a lot of ways. I think if it is going to be successful, it has to be everyone's business – and thus has to be 'real' in many of the day to day functions of people's roles. Each team member should be able to talk at some level about how they contribute to helping students to stay. I think interactions with students about why they are here and how they can persist need to be personal and demonstrate the highest level of care. It can't just be one more thing that people have to do – that extra thing that someone added to their job. Just as the college student experience is a holistic one (involving both the inside of class-room learning and outside of classroom learning), keeping and retaining a student must also involve all areas associated with the student experience. Being able to identify students who may be at-retention-risk and then being able to collaborate with fellow administrators or faculty (when appropriate) about how each can best help a student allows issues and concerns to be addressed intentionally and individually where possible. I would also say that you cannot only rely on the high-tech efforts – it really has to go beyond just emailing, calling, or texting. Those high-tech pieces are important, no doubt, but I would think they should be a piece of the strategy – not the primary strategy. I think that success in retention comes from the personal commitment to each student (individually) mattering. Personal contact, interpersonal concern, and connection with students is, I think one of the key components to helping students believe that they can overcome obstacles and thus remain and persist. I think as you look at developing and coordinating a team, examining where those personal connections are and can be made is important. As a housing team member, I think I would be remiss if I did not say that I think a retention team should definitely involve residential living and learning team members at some level. Your residential living and learning team members can be a critical part of your retention strategy. They can often go and find or make contact with students when no other form of contact may be working. Finally, I think having a comprehensive method for reporting (and evaluating) information from various partners to allow for the constructing of a comprehensive picture of the student is important. Here we have the electronic retention tool that members of the retention group use to track information about follow-ups, etc. Having a common place for campus partners to contribute to the conversation - what information is coming from their CA (about being homesick), what information may be coming from their academic advisor, what information may be coming from the Conduct Office, from their instructors – all of the various pieces make only a piece of a larger picture of the student and their experience. It allows you to be very intentional in strategy applied because the strategy that you may be applying to one student may be completely ineffective for another.

INITIATIVE 10
UTILIZING TECHNOLOGY

Technology plays a significant role in the University's efforts in creating, disseminating, and utilizing retention data. A member from the Department of Information Technology (IT) serves on the University's Retention Advisory Board. The Board receives daily automated retention reports for the current cohort after all course registration windows have opened. Furthermore, the Board has access to Tableau where members can view retention rates based on numerous variables (e.g., residence hall, major, ethnicity, etc.). The Board uses this data to be both proactive and reactive in their retention endeavors. Front-line campus professionals also rely heavily on technology as it relates to retention. The Department of Information Technology has been critical in supporting retention by creating an online retention tool for documenting and sharing information. Professionals from across campus use the online tool to make retention-related notes and share them with

> The Department of Information Technology has been critical in supporting retention by creating an online retention tool for documenting and sharing information.

others on campus. This tool has not only helped us quickly address persistence barriers, but it also has improved our efficiency. Once a student states that he/she is not returning and the tool is updated, no one else on campus continues to contact the student encouraging him/her to return. Other important technological components that IT has developed to assist our retention efforts include: Freshman Attendance Based Initiative (FABI portal), attendance scanners in classrooms, online student grade information, and an at-risk flag that faculty and staff can electronically raise for students of concern. The University of Mississippi is fortunate to have an IT Department that supports retention and is willing to help whenever possible.

The Department of Information Technology has been instrumental in supporting the University's retention efforts.

Information Technology Representative on the Retention Advisory Board

The University of Mississippi's Retention Advisory Board (RAB) inclusion of a member from IT should not go unnoticed. Technology is a key component to many successful initiatives on a college campus, and retention should be no different. When a retention group includes a representative from Institutional Research (Initiative 4) and someone from IT, there is no reason that data cannot be successfully obtained, shared, and acted upon by the institution. The University of Mississippi's RAB representative from IT is very engaged in retention conversations and actively explores ways technology can support current and new initiatives.

Before the RAB had an IT representative, we would brainstorm ways to help freshmen persist, and if it involved IT we were hopeful that IT would support our efforts. This was not always the case, as some ideas discussed by the group were not feasible for IT to develop, maintain, and/or operate. However, once an IT representative was officially part of the group, this person could either (a) tell us if the proposal was feasible, or (b) give us technical input before addressing the possibilities with IT leadership. From understanding how certain programs function to why current capabilities are able to be expanded, IT's role on the Board has made us more informed and saved us valuable time in our efforts.

Thinking back to when an IT representative first became involved with the board, I am not sure why we never had an official member when we first started the Retention Steering Committee. Based upon my recollection, we asked the IT Director of Application Development to temporarily join our meetings as we discussed possible third-party retention software solutions. Anyone who works with retention knows there are numerous third-party vendors who offer to solve an institution's retention problem. The University's RAB decided to explore several options, and if we found one that would positively impact freshman retention, the group would submit a proposal to the provost advocating for the purchase of the software. After attending vendor presentations at conferences focused on online research, the RAB decided to invite three companies to present on campus. However, before these on-campus presentations took place, the RAB recognized the importance of inviting someone from IT to attend. The University of Mississippi uses unique campus management software and the RAB was concerned that a potential third-party vendor's product would not be easily adaptable to our system. The RAB knew what type of data and services we needed from a retention solution, but openly acknowledged that our expertise of the technical aspects was rather limited. Therefore, the representative from IT attended each vendor presentation. This person's presence was very beneficial, as after the RAB finished asking our service-related questions, the IT representative would inquire about the technical and compatibility aspects. Once the three presentations concluded and the IT representative was able to provide valuable feedback, the RAB decided to make this person a permanent member from the retention group. The RAB did recommend a product to be purchased and submitted a proposal to the provost. Unfortunately, leadership at the University opted not to purchase the recommended solution. However, because an IT representative was included in the presentations, this person was able to gain a better understanding of the value of these products. This person's knowledge and support was invaluable when the University's IT Department offered to create a retention tool that could perform some of the components the RAB emphasized during the third-party demonstrations.

Specific Technology Utilized at the University

It is extremely important to have a representative from IT included in a retention group. However, understanding the actual technology utilized in retention efforts is just as vital. Some of the technological retention-related tools the University of Mississippi's IT Department has been involved with includes: online retention tool, Tableau software, Freshman Attendance Based Intervention (FABI) system, and student grade information. The work IT has performed regarding student success and retention projects has been greatly appreciated by front-line professionals who use their tools when working with students.

Online Retention Tool

Despite not having a catchy name, the University of Mississippi's online Freshman Cohort Retention Tool has been an asset to retention efforts. Although the University did not select a third-party retention solution, IT asked the RAB to select some of the primary attributes from each system, so it could develop a retention product for on-campus usage. One of the features the RAB advocated for was the ability to share retention-related notes with colleagues across campus. Prior to the retention tool becoming available, numerous Excel files were shared via e-mail. Academic advisors would add notes to a central spreadsheet, then this document would be sent to Financial Aid so they could work with the freshmen who stated they were having financial issues. Meanwhile, the document could have been sent to Housing so student or profes-

Can be contacted.

student number	**JEREMY DOE**
school	**COLLEGE OF LIBERAL ARTS**
program	**B.S. in Biology**
schedule	**Spring Schedule** **Fall Schedule**
standing	**GOOD**
ethnicity	**Black or African American**
gender	**M**
resident	**Yes**
cellphone	**000-000-0000**
email	**jdoe@olemis.edu**
external email	
home address	**000 STREET NAME** **PERFECTVILLE, MS 30000**
local address	**PO BOX 1848** **UNIVERSITY, MS 38677**

9116 - Accounts Receivable Hold $0.50

mother	**JOHNETTE DOE**
phone	**000-000-0000**
email	**jdoe@email.com**
ferpa	**Academic** **Accounting** **Financial Aid**

other	**JOHN DOE**
phone	**000-000-0000**
email	**jJdoe@email.com**
ferpa	**No Academic** **No Accounting** **No Financial Aid**

Set contact status for this student.

Any choice other than "can be contacted" will mark the student as "do not contact." Please be as specific as possible.

Can be contacted.

Send email notification.

Enter email addresses separated by commas.

Add a note about this student.

Submit

Freshman Cohort Retention Tool

Note: Scrolling may be required to view all displayed columns

Show / hide columns

Show [25 ⌄] entries

Search: _____

Number ▲	Last	First	Program (Type to filter) ✕	Spring (Select value) ⬍ ✕	Fall (Select value) ⬍ ✕	Holds (Select value) ⬍ ✕	Contact (Select value) ⬍ ✕	Status (Type to filter) ✕
125	Doe	John	B.S. in Integrated Marketing Communicat.	Yes	Yes	No	Yes	Can be contacted.
124	Doe	James	B.A. in Classics	Yes	Yes	No	Yes	Can be contacted.
125	Doe	Jacelyn	B.S. in Biology	Yes	Yes	Yes	Yes	Can be contacted.
126	Doe	Jamie	Undeclared	Yes	Yes	No	Yes	Can be contacted.
127	Doe	Jasmine	B.S.Ch.E. in Chemical Engineering	Yes	Yes	No	Yes	Can be contacted.
129	Doe	Jessica	Business	Yes	Yes	No	Yes	Can be contacted.
130	Doe	Joshua	B.S. in Pharmaceutical Sciences	Yes	Yes	No	Yes	Can be contacted.
131	Doe	Jacob	B.S. in Physics	No	Yes	No	Yes	Can be contacted.
132	Doe	Jackson	B.Accy. in Accountancy	No	Yes	No	Yes	Can be contacted.
133	Doe	Jim	B.A. in Biology	Yes	Yes	Yes	Yes	Can be contacted.
134	Doe	Jenessa	Undeclared	Yes	Yes	Yes	Yes	Can be contacted.
135	Doe	Jeremy	B.A. in Biology	No	Yes	No	Yes	Can be contacted.
136	Doe	Janet	B.S. in Pharmaceutical Sciences	Yes	Yes	No	Yes	Can be contacted.
137	Doe	Janet	B.Accy. in Accountancy	Yes	Yes	No	Yes	Can be contacted.
138	Doe	Jason	B.A. in Public Policy Leadership	Yes	Yes	No	Yes	Can be contacted.
139	Doe	Jimmy	B.S. in Integrated Marketing Communicat.	Yes	Yes	No	Yes	Can be contacted.
140	Doe	Josceph	B.E. in Engineering	Yes	Yes	No	Yes	Can be contacted.
141	Doe	Julian	B.S. in Pharmaceutical Sciences	Yes	Yes	No	Yes	Can be contacted.
142	Doe	Judith	B.A. in English Education	Yes	Yes	No	Yes	Can be contacted.
143	Doe	Jonathan	B.A. in Mathematics	Yes	Yes	No	Yes	Can be contacted.
144	Doe	Joanna	B.A. in Biochemistry	Yes	Yes	Yes	Yes	Can be contacted.
145	Doe	Julianna	B.S.C.J. in Criminal Justice	No	Yes	No	Yes	Can be contacted.
146	Doe	Jennifer	B.S. in Pharmaceutical Sciences	Yes	Yes	No	Yes	Can be contacted.
147	Doe	Josh	B.A. in Biology	Yes	Yes	No	Yes	Can be contacted.
148	Doe	Judy	B.A. in English	Yes	Yes	Yes	Yes	Can be contacted.

Number	Last	First	Program	Spring	Fall	Holds	Contact	Status

Showing 1 to 25 of 3,855 entries

◀ Previous | Next ▶

sional staff members could seek out freshmen who had no notes on the spreadsheet. Or the Office of Conflict Resolution may have received a small subset of the document including freshmen who had a student conduct hold and had not registered for classes. Needless to say, with so many lists floating around the RAB knew this was not the most efficient approach. Based on conversations with colleagues at other institutions, some retention communication and documentation is still captured and shared using this method.

In 2014 when the retention tool was first made available, it was easy to see that documentation and note-sharing was dramatically improved. For example, if Financial Aid was working with a student who said his/her parents plan to pay off the balance at the end of the month and the note was made in the retention tool, other campus professionals (e.g., academic advisor, EDHE instructor, etc.) would not continue to contact the student to inquire why he/she had not registered for classes. Additionally, these notes are more secure than e-mailing an Excel file, as the retention tool can only be accessed by authorized professionals, who must log into his/her myOleMiss account to access the tool. Furthermore, individuals with access can add and view notes at any time from any device with Internet capabilities.

Another important feature that was requested was the ability to categorize why a freshman was leaving the University. On the old Excel spreadsheets, the Center for Student Success and First-Year Experience's assistant director-retention would have to create separate tabs by departure category which listed the student's information and notes related to his/her reason(s) for leaving. The online retention tool has 12 pre-populated reasons for a lack of persistence in which a campus professional may chose. The reasons include: Not returning due to monetary reasons, grades, distance from home/homesickness, social fit, admission to another school, health/medical issues, personal/family issues, legal/disciplinary reasons, major fit, athletic reasons, military orders, and other. Almost all freshmen who leave are able to be classified under one of the pre-populated reasons. In the rare case a reason does not fall under our pre-populated choices, campus professionals can select "other," but need to provide

The more information you have about a student, the more you can help complete the retention picture.

adequate notes. Disney internships and touring with a choir in Africa are two recent examples that would fall under the "other" category. Once a reason is selected, the system automatically changes the student to "Do Not Contact." This message is important as it indicates the University is aware of the student's plans and representatives from the institution do not need to continue contacting the student. Anyone who verifies that a student is not returning must also include notes regarding specifics of the conversation. For example, if an academic advisor selects "Social Fit" as the primary reason the student is leaving the University, the notes section may contain a note similar to "Per an e-mail from the student, Student's Name indicated the he/she had trouble making friends and was going to transfer to New Institution's Name where some of his/her high school friends attend." Or a staff member from Financial Aid may select "Financial Concerns" as the reason for departure. The notes section may contain something along the lines of "Per phone conversations with Parent's Name, Student's Name will be transferring to a school back home where he/she will receive in-state tuition. The family cannot afford to continue paying out-of-state tuition." With the ability to categorize reasons students cite for leaving the University, communication efforts are more efficient and data is easily accessible.

The third attribute the RAB wanted from the online tool was a student dashboard. The dashboard would have key information about the student. The RAB brainstormed the most important pieces of information and submitted a list to IT. After several prototypes, IT was able to get the requested information in an easily viewable format. Some of the information that is on the student dashboard includes: student's photo, local and home addresses, all e-mail addresses, cell phone number, parent/guardian information and permissions, holds, upcoming academic schedules, academic standing, GPA, balance owed, and retention notes. Campus professionals can access important information in a one-stop dashboard view when working with a student. Retention often is a complex puzzle and having information such as balance owed, residency, academic standing, and GPA can provide insight to a student's situation before the staff member is able to make contact. Additionally, retention notes from the previous semester also can provide useful information. In the fall if a student stated health concerns may prevent him/her from returning, but decided to return to the University for the spring, it is not unreasonable for the staff member to consider that possible health issues may still be a potential risk for the student. The more information you have about a student, the more you can help complete the retention picture. Of course, the best information will come directly from the student or family member, but any information obtained is useful. IT's work in developing the online retention tool has been greatly appreciated and has made a major impact on the University's efficiency.

Online Retention Tool's Integration with Tableau

As previously mentioned in Initiative 4, the University's Office of Institutional Research, Effectiveness, and Planning (IREP) uses Tableau to manage retention data. In 2015, IT was able to sync information from the online retention tool to retention data in Tableau. Now, reasons for not returning are linked to the Tableau data. This linkage provides an extra level of data for exploration. For example, I can use Tableau to view non-residents from California, who live in a specific residence hall, and are on academic probation. The online retention tool could then take that list and tell me how many did not return to the University and cited "financial concerns" or "distance from home" as their primary reasons for leaving. The amount and types of data we now have access to is unprecedented.

In the short time these two applications have been linked, we have been able to see a variety of benefits. Data is more accessible, upper-level administrators can view retention data using an assortment of criteria, IREP's retention workload has decreased, and we better understand retention from a holistic point-of-view. Furthermore, front-line professionals who are involved in student persistence, are avid users of the online retention tool. When we take their work from the tool and show them

how it is used in the bigger picture when combined with Tableau information, it reinforces the valuable role they play in our retention efforts. The University is grateful that we have capable professionals in IREP and IT who value retention and work well together. Without them

The Department of Information Technology is located in Powers Hall.

understanding our retention culture and being supportive of our efforts, I am not sure they would have been as successful in their collaboration. I am excited about what the future holds regarding continuous updates to this initiative, as well as other opportunities for IREP and IT to partner on projects that support freshman retention.

Freshman Attendance Based Initiative (FABI)

The University of Mississippi's Freshman Attendance Based Initiative (FABI) was discussed in Initiative 9. However, this system would not be in existence if it were not for the early work and continual updates from IT. The original online reporting structure allowed for instructors to log into their myOleMiss accounts to report absences in each course taught. Instructors were directed to report absences once a student missed the course three times and every time thereafter, as each additional absence caused more campus professionals to be added to the communication model. IT did an excellent job in creating the instructor reporting portal and the FABI coordinator's data collection system. This program worked well as long as instructors reported absences and professionals in the communication model (e.g., advisors, housing staff, etc.) utilized the data for student intervention.

As the University's enrollment has grown, it became obvious that attendance tracking needed to become a more automated process. In 2013, IT began piloting attendance scanners in some classrooms on campus. Students had to swipe their student ID cards through the scanners in order to verify their attendance. Instructors could choose to turn on the scanners for their courses. If an instructor opted to utilize the attendance scanner, he/she had to attend a training session. Instructors could set the time parameters in which scanners would be activated. For example, the scanner may be active 10 minutes before class begins and turn off five minutes after the class begins. Therefore, students had to be cognizant not to swipe too early and not be late; otherwise, they would not get credit for attending. Once the scanners were proven to be effective, they were synced to the FABI system. This synchronization significantly increased the number of students reported through the FABI system.

Each year additional scanners are added throughout the University. In 2015, there were 62 classrooms equipped with attendance scanners.

With most rooms having scanners the campus professional who coordinates FABI has become overwhelmed with all the reports. To further complicate the system, the attendance data is not as accurate as it was when manually reported. Many instructors activate the scanners to track attendance during the first two weeks of classes when the University has a mandatory policy for attendance reporting. However, some instructors do not turn off the scanners, but inform the students they are no longer taking attendance. This scenario causes numerous students to be reported with three or more absences and appear on FABI communication lists. However, when the students are contacted, they state the professor informed them they do not have to scan for that specific class. Needless to say, the FABI coordinator and professionals in the communication model become frustrated after contacting students who have not been absent from class. Other complications include professors who cancel class, but do not turn off the scanner, students who lose their ID cards and the instructor manually records their attendance, but it is not logged in the scanner system, and the occasional ID card discrepancy. Although the scanner system has been helpful in keeping up with growth at the University and in mandatory reporting during the first two weeks, I am not confident it has benefited FABI. This effectiveness of FABI will continue to be explored. We will determine whether adjustments or possibly discontinuing the program would be our best option.

Student Grade Information

The ability for students to access their grades online is important. IT plays an important role in this service, as students have two different ways to view their grades. The first option, which is our Blackboard system, allows students to receive frequent updates regarding their graded homework, quizzes, tests, etc. All professors have the option to utilize Blackboard as an academic resource for their classes. Specifically, related to this section, the grade book feature can keep students up-to-date on where they stand in a specific course. Unfortunately, the utilization of Blackboard is not required by the University, so not all instructors activate Blackboard for their courses. However, for those who do active the system and use it efficiently, it can be very beneficial for students. Another good example of IT's support for student success is when staff created the ability for select campus professionals (e.g., academic advisors, athletic academic advisors, etc.) to have access to students' grades in Blackboard. As academic advisors are working with students to plan their upcoming semester, they are unaware of the students' final grades. Therefore, by reviewing grades in Blackboard, the advisor and student can have a meaningful conversation on how the semester may end academically. Athletic academic advisors can use this function in a similar capacity to an academic advisor, but also can know current grades for athletic eligibility purposes.

In the First-Year Experience Course (EDHE 105) we ask that all instructors use Blackboard. This request not only helped the students enrolled in the course, but also provided EDHE 105 instructors the opportunity to assist new freshmen in navigating the Blackboard system. In 2015, we required all EDHE 105 instructors to spend a class session covering important technology components that new freshmen need to understand. The components include: University of Mississippi e-mail (and how to sync to students' smart phones), myOleMiss accounts, and Blackboard (including requiring all students to download the Blackboard application). Instructors are provided training on all these services prior to the beginning of the semester. We are hopeful that educating our freshmen early regarding these online tools will benefit them throughout their educational journey at the University.

The other online option for students to view grades is through their myOleMiss account. Unlike Blackboard, grades in myOleMiss are only updated twice a semester. The first viewing occurs after mid-terms. The Registrar sets the date for mid-term grades to be submitted. All instructors of 100- and 200-level courses are required to submit mid-term grades. One unique aspect about mid-term grades for freshmen is that absences from FABI and the attendance scanners are linked to mid-term grades. Therefore, if an advisor or parent, sees that a student has a "D" in a course and six absences at mid-term, a conversation about the importance of class attendance can occur. Viewing final grades online is similar to mid-terms. The Registrar assigns the due date for final grades, which usually is the Monday following final exam week. Attendance information is not recorded on final grades. Students who complete their teacher evaluations can view their final grades one day before their peers who opted not to participate in the evaluation process.

Parents have access to students' grades in their myOleMiss accounts. Students have the option of allowing their parents to create a Parent Web ID. The Parent Web ID allows some access to a student's myOleMiss account. If access is granted and a Parent Web ID is created, parents can view a student's grades (only in myOleMiss, not in Blackboard), holds, class schedule, financial information, and pay the Bursar bill. In my opinion, the Parent Web ID has been an important tool in keeping some of our freshmen on track. Having both University professionals and parents striving to achieve the same goal (i.e., helping the freshman be successful) is paramount to our retention efforts. IT staff have done a remarkable job in supporting students, faculty, staff, and others through their willingness to listen to the needs of their customers and the value they place on student success, satisfaction, and persistence.

Utilizing Technology

Think about how technology is currently utilized in your retention efforts.

Who are the direct retention-related points of contact in the Department of Information Technology?

_____

_____

_____

What types of retention-related support do they provide?

_____

_____

How does their involvement benefit freshman retention?

_____

_____

Brainstorm ways to further include technology in retention efforts.

_____

_____

_____

_____

INTERVIEW

Chris Reichley

Director of Application Development and Integration

Describe your role in the University's retention efforts.

I serve on the Retention Advisory Board as a representative of the Information Technology department. As the Director of the Applications Development and Integration department, my specific contributions include planning and implementation of applications and processes within the university's student information system to support retention efforts and improve efficiency and tracking.

In your opinion, what are some of the most effective retention strategies at the University?

In recent years we have improved the sharing and centralization of information among departments working with retention. This has allowed for a more seamless partnership between these groups so that efforts are not duplicated and wasted. We have also implemented an automated attendance tracking system to remove bookkeeping burdens from the faculty and allow for recording in high seat classrooms where it was previously not feasible. This information is then used to follow-up with at risk students before they reach a point of no return.

Since you became involved in the University's retention efforts, describe some changes you have observed.

A tighter and more focused approach for the overall retention efforts has been developed. Communication has been improved between different offices paired with improved access to real time information on students and factors that impede their ability to continue at the university. This helps the university improve the utility of its resources and ultimately the number of students they can aid in retention related efforts.

Where do you see retention efforts going in the short term? Long term?

Currently, I see our university moving in the direction of richer analytics and data analysis. We have recently expanded our technology infrastructure giving us opportunities to further leverage our student system and the large volume of data it holds. By moving from a reactive to a more predictive analytics model, we will be able to identify students at risk earlier and take action to improve our overall rate of student success. These efforts will also help us to more accurately assess the effectiveness of existing retention and student success related initiatives.

What advice would you give other institutions regarding their retention efforts?

Do not be discouraged by the numbers. There are many factors outside of the university control that will cause fluctuations up and down over the course of years. Watch broader trends and remember that retention is a balancing act with admissions and other university goals. Improve communication and buy in from the various departments that can and will have an impact on retention, quite often the varying point of views will bring to light previously unconsidered areas for improvement.

INITIATIVE 11
ACADEMIC SUPPORT

Each student who begins the journey through higher education should have one primary goal: to earn his/her degree. Some students will be well-prepared and easily navigate their path to degree completion. However, others will need more assistance, which could be in the form of academic support. Student who do well academically, either on their own or with the help of institutional support, are more likely to persist when compared to peers who are doing poorly. Although the ultimate objective is for students to graduate and earn their degrees, my goal at the University of Mississippi (and for those reading this book) is to assist freshmen in persisting from year one to year two. That is why I am grateful my institution understands the importance of providing academic support and has created specific initiatives, courses, programs, and policies to help students achieve academic success.

The Importance of Academic Support

There are many reasons an institution of higher education should offer academic support opportunities to students. From the easy answer of "it is the right thing to do," to the more complex view of "intricacies relating good grades to campus connections," the fundamental principle that students with better grades persist and graduate at higher levels than those who perform poorly on their academics, remains at the core. For the purpose of this book, I will highlight four reasons which I have experience with, as they relate to why it is important to offer academic support.

Students with good grades persist at higher levels

Each semester when we have freshmen, who choose to leave the University, I look to see if they were in "Good Standing, Academic Probation, or Academic Suspension." Although we do lose some who are in good standing, the percentages of those who are on academic probation or suspension and choose to leave, are greater. Other factors should be considered, but I acknowledge that being in poor academic standing is not going to help a student's case to return to the University. However, if a student is in good standing and had a positive academic experience, he/she may be more capable of overcoming the other issues, with a notation of academic success being a positive factor, in his/her return.

From my experience, it appears students who do well academically have fewer non-academic issues. I realize this is a broad stereotype and every student does not fall under this statement, but when I hear of freshmen who leave and cite legal/disciplinary issues, financial concerns, and similar reasons for departure, many of them also have low GPAs. On the other hand, freshmen who have at least a 2.5 GPA during the freshman year seem to have fewer non-academic issues. Although I do not have the data, I also believe that as the GPA increases, the number of non-academic issues decreases. Again, this is solely based on my experience working in freshman retention, in which a handful of cases on either end of the spectrum could be cited. For example, an Honors College freshman could have legal disciplinary issues and leave the institution, just as a marginal 2.0 student could maintain a "C" average (i.e., minimum required to remain in good academic standing), never have any non-academic issues and graduate in four years. At the end of the day, freshmen who do well academically and experience success during the first year, will persist and graduate at higher levels than their peers who got off on the wrong foot in the classroom.

Freshmen who do well academically and experience success during the first year will persist and graduate at higher levels than their peers who got off on the wrong foot in the classroom.

The ability to keep scholarships/financial aid

As previously mentioned in other initiatives, a significant number of freshmen who leave the University of Mississippi cite "financial concerns" as the primary reason for their departure. Whether students need a specific GPA to maintain their scholarships, apply for new awards, or qualify for various types of financial aid, academic success can influence the results, and have an impact on students remaining at the institution. If a student is doing well and maintaining the needed GPA to keep his/her financial aid, that is one less issue to worry about in the world of retention. However, if a student performs poorly in the classroom, and loses his/her financial aid, from a retention perspective, you have to not only worry about the ripple effect from poor grades, the financial loss also will be a factor in a lack of persistence.

If students do not meet the requirements to keep scholarships after the first year, they may appeal. Although there is no guarantee an appeal committee, coordinated by the Office of Financial Aid, will grant the student's appeal, I do know students will have a better chance if they were close to the required GPA, understand what went wrong, and have a good plan going forward. For many scholarships offered through the University, students must maintain a 3.0 GPA. Therefore, if students come up slightly short (e.g., 2.9), they may be more likely to win their appeal as opposed to student who appeal with a 1.0 GPA. The shared knowledge of appeals to front-line professionals such as academic advisors and FYE instructors, is an asset to our retention efforts. When a student is feeling frustrated with a low grade in a course, encouragement from a campus professional to continue striving and to develop an academic success plan for the course, may be the difference in a "C" versus a "D," which could impact how close a student is to the 3.0 GPA requirement. Additionally, informing students that if they take a summer course or two and do well, it will be factored into the Appeals Committee's decision.

Finally, the one-time retention funds that were mentioned in a previous initiative do have GPA considerations. The Office of Financial Aid is very selective in whom it chooses to award retention funds. Therefore, if a freshman falls upon hard times financially, he may be more likely to receive some help if he has a good GPA. Furthermore, the amount may be raised or lowered based on academic performance. For example, if a freshman was $3,000 short of paying her prior semester tuition, Financial Aid may award the entire amount if she had a 4.0 GPA, as this would be considered a good investment. However, if the student only had a 2.5 GPA, Financial Aid may offer one-time funds of $1,500, but it will be disbursed only after the student has paid the initial $1,500. For freshmen with less than a 2.0 GPA, there is little hope of qualifying for one-time retention funds. We are hopeful freshmen who receive scholarships or other types of financial aid fulfill their academic requirements and seamlessly persist on to year two. However, anyone who works in freshman retention understands that not all students will earn the required GPA and that financial considerations may compound academic issues. Therefore, when financial issues come into play, every letter grade matters. The encouragement of students to do the best they can in every course could come into play in more ways than one.

Gain memberships into campus organizations

It is no secret that freshmen who are connected to the institution are more likely to persist. The University of Mississippi has several hundred campus organizations, including many fraternities and sororities. There is a strong Greek Life culture at the University. Many of these organizations have GPA requirements in order for students to gain membership and actively participate. With a large number of freshmen participating in fraternities and sororities, we are hopeful that all students have a good experience, while making their grades so they can remain in good standing with the organization. Unfortunately, each year we hear of students who leave the University because they were unable to remain in their organization. If students utilize academic support resources as a way to earn good grades so they are able to remain active in their organizations, then the University's retention rates will benefit.

It is no secret that freshmen who are connected to the institution are more likely to persist.

Parents are more supportive when higher grades are achieved

Parents are a valuable resource when it comes to an institution retaining students. In my opinion, parents should be seen as allies who share the same goal as the institution. In my 12 years of working at the University, I have interacted with parents who were at both ends of the spectrum when it comes to how involved they were in their child's first year at the University. Some parents contacted me over trivial issues, while others' reasons for communication were easily justified. On the other end of the scale, we have had students who were struggling with academics, social life, health issues, and other matters that we did not find out about until it was too late. Had their parents informed me or another campus professional (preferably someone who was involved in our retention initiatives) we could have potentially assisted before it was too late. Overall, I welcome parent interactions because you never know when they may reveal a persistence issue. And as anyone who works regularly in student retention can attest, every student counts when it comes to retention rates.

One commonality I have found when working with parents regarding the decision to allow their child to return for a second year, is that those who have freshmen with good grades are more likely to allow students to return. For example, if a freshman gets in trouble and receives a disciplinary strike, we may worry that his parents may want him to transfer home at the end of the semester. When University staff members begin our retention efforts, we would inquire as to why the student is not returning if he had not registered for the upcoming semester. Based on my experience, parents of a freshman, who has a 3.0 GPA, in this scenario, would be more likely to allow their student to return when compared to parents of a freshman who earned a 1.0 GPA.

Another good example is social fit or distance from home as factors for potential lack of persistence. I have heard from parents who say their freshman wants to transfer due to not finding his/her social niche, or wanting to move back closer to local friends and family. When this occurs, I am hopeful the parents are of the mindset that the child staying at the University of Mississippi is the best choice (another reason to see them as allies). Based on my experience, if the student is doing well academically, the parents often acknowledge that they prefer their child to stay at the University. However, if the student is doing poorly, they usually admit it is in their child's best interest to leave the University. Coincidentally, some of these parents attempt to correlate the student's poor grades to some aspect of the University in which they are unhappy (e.g., Housing, Greek Life, etc.). Overall, I can confidentially state that I would much rather interact with a parent of a freshman who has good grades when it comes to student persistence.

Academic Support Initiatives

At the University of Mississippi there is a wide array of academic support opportunities afforded to our students. The University understands that we must provide adequate academic resources in order to help our students be successful. For the purposes of this book, I will highlight several initiatives that are available to most students, but we specifically target freshmen to utilize them as another mechanism in our retention efforts. The resources I will address include: academic consultations, tutor identification, Supplemental Instruction (SI), reactive support courses, forgiveness policy, and programs that address courses with high "D" and "F" grade rates.

Academic consultations

The Center for Student Success and First-Year Experience's (CSS-FYE) Academic Support Programs unit offers a variety of support options. One of these programs includes academic consultations. Students can request to have consultations as often as needed. Academic consultations are conducted by a professional staff member or a graduate assistant who is employed through the CSSFYE. Consultations can address a variety of issues, but it is important to note that this is not tutoring for a specific course. Traditionally, the consultations involve the staff member or the graduate assistant helping the student develop a plan for academic success. This is accomplished by looking at the student's schedule and creating a plan of action for each course. Using a semester calendar they can identify the most appropriate ways and times to study, utilize campus resources, and offer additional accountability, if the student believes she may not be able to stick to the plan. Other types of consultations may focus on a specific academic success skill. Examples of these types of consultations could include time management, note-taking, or preparing for tests. In most cases the students initiate the consultations. However, we have had parents who were concerned about their child's academic progress, so we would recommend that parents encourage their child to make an appointment for a consultation.

Tutoring/tutoring clearinghouse

Tutoring at the University of Mississippi is very decentralized. Some schools (e.g., Engineering, Pharmacy, etc.) offer free tutoring in various subjects for their majors. Additionally, we have a few departments (Math, Writing & Rhetoric, etc.) that offer free tutoring to any student enrolled in their courses. The Center for Student Success and First-Year Experience's Academic Support Programs (ASP) coordinate a tutoring clearinghouse. At the beginning of each semester a staff member contacts each department on campus and asks for the name and contact information of a department staff member who could help identify tutors. This list is kept on the ASP website. Some departments such as Math, who receive numerous requests, identify several potential tutors early in the semester and allow us to post those students' contact information directly to the website. This way students who need a math tutor do not have to go through the department to acquire the information. However,

Tutors are very important in helping students understand complicated material.

for most subjects, making contact with the department representative is the required method. For example, if a student is looking for an art history tutor, he can find the art/art history staff member's information and make contact regarding a tutor. The staff member may send the student one or more names of potential tutors, in which the student could contact the individual(s) directly. The University has no official obligations to the tutoring agreements, regarding time, location, price, or expectations, so any arrangements that are agreed upon by the student and the tutor are outside the University's scope of jurisdiction.

Supplemental Instruction (SI)

Supplemental Instruction (SI) was introduced at the University of Mississippi in 2010 as a free service to support students in courses with high "D" and "F" grade rates. SI is a form of tutoring, but not in the traditional sense. In the SI sessions, a former student who did well in the course attends the lectures, then offers weekly help sessions to recap the material and offer additional support on difficult concepts. Additionally, students who attend SI sessions can share notes, prepare for upcoming tests, and form study groups. During the pilot year, SI was offered for three courses: Accy 201, Bisc 160, and Chem 105. In Fall 2015, those same three courses offered SI, but four new courses have been added: Bisc 102, Bisc 206, Chem 101, and Math 261. I am pleased that SI has been effective and continues to expand. Hopefully, more courses will utilize SI in the future.

Support courses

EDHE 105 "First Year Experience" was previously mentioned in this book. I consider this course the proactive course for new freshmen. If freshmen find themselves on academic probation after their first semester, they are required to take the reactive course EDHE 101, "Academic

Skills for College." EDHE 101, a three-hour, letter-graded course that addresses study skills and academic success, was mentioned in Initiative 1. The other reactive support course, that is part of the Contractual Re-admission Program (also referenced in Initiative 1), is EDHE 202, "Fundamentals of Active Learning." EDHE 202 is a two-hour, letter-graded course. Students in EDHE 202 meet individually or in a small group with a graduate student and have other requirements such as study hours. Freshmen who are placed on academic suspension after their first year, and who are readmitted after applying to the CRP, must enroll in EDHE 202. One new addition to both EDHE 101 and 202 occurred during the Spring 2016 semester. The course supervisor coordinated with Dr. Ken Sufka, Psychology faculty member and author of The A Game, to give presentations to students taking EDHE 101 and 202. The A Game is dis-

Dr. Ken Sufka, author of
The A Game, speaks to a class.

tributed to all new freshmen and students in EDHE 202. The book focuses on nine essential steps to earning good grades. Dr. Sufka's presentation early in the semester helps students understand where they may have made mistakes in the past, and offers them advice on how to right the ship academically. Student feedback regarding Dr. Sufka's presentation and class discussion about the book was very positive. Plans to utilize Dr. Sufka's book and his presentation for this at-risk population will hopefully be a permanent addition to these courses. Unrelated to freshman retention, but important to point out, the University now offers EDHE 305, "Transfer Year Experience," and EDHE 303, "Academic Skills for Transfer Students," in efforts to support our transfer students the same way EDHE 105 and 101 support our freshmen.

Forgiveness Policy

The Forgiveness Policy at the University of Mississippi allows students to forgive up to four poor grades during their undergraduate careers. The grades of C-, D, and F are the only ones that qualify for the forgiveness policy. After a student makes one of the aforementioned grades, he/she must re-enroll for the course at the University. In order to use forgiveness, the course must be taken at the University of Mississippi, but can be taken in a different format (e.g., traditional vs. online), and can be taken with a different instructor. Once the new grade is earned, the student will complete a Grade Forgiveness Form and submit it to the Registrar's Office. Although the first course attempt will continue to be displayed on the student's transcript, the old grade will have an "R" listed next to it, and not be factored into the student's Resident GPA. The forgiveness policy is very popular among freshmen who may have been overwhelmed during their first year, unaware of how difficult a course was going to be, or subject to any other factor that contributed to them earning a bad grade. Regardless of the reason, students (and their parents) appreciate that the University will allow them to remove a poor grade and not have a rough academic start derail an entire academic career.

High "D" and "F" course initiatives

When attempting to address retention issues, it is not uncommon for institutions to examine courses with high "D" and "F" rates and/or gateway courses that cause barriers for a large number of students. When the University's Retention Advisory Board reviewed freshman courses with high "D" and "F" rates there were two that stood out. They were Bisc 160 and Chem 105. These are the required first-year, first-semester biology and chemistry courses for science majors, some engineering majors, health professions (e.g., medicine, dentistry, pharmacy, etc.), and other select majors. The lecture sections for the courses were large and moved at a fast pace. Some students were underprepared for these courses, while other students did not fully understand how to prepare and study for these courses. One early attempt to address student success in these courses was to implement a required math ACT/SAT sub score. If students do not have the appropriate sub score, they can take a pre-requisite such as Chem 101 or Math 125. If the student makes the required grade in the pre-requisite, he/she is welcome to take the courses in the future. The required sub score or completion of the pre-requisite has prevented underprepared students from enrolling and the success rates in the courses have increased.

The previously mentioned course policy change is one way to ensure success in difficult courses. However, I appreciate the "hands on" helpful approach that each department took in addressing low grades in their courses. The Department of Biology created Biology Bootcamp. Biology Bootcamp is a five-day preparation program that occurs the week before the fall semester begins. The goal of the program is to prepare new freshmen who are enrolled in Bisc 160 for the fall to do well in the course. Bootcamp gives participants a head start in understanding what is expected in the course, as well as getting them acclimated with campus resources and faculty members in the biology department. The Department of Chemistry and Biochemistry also came up with an interesting concept that has proven to be effective. It offers Chem 105 students the Parachute Program. In the Parachute Program students who are enrolled in Chem 105 and fail the first exam, may "parachute" down to Chem 101. Chem 101 is a survey course, which is taught at a slower pace and lags behind Chem 105 by about two weeks. Therefore, if students need to drop down to Chem 101, they are not behind peers who began in the course, do not get a poor grade in Chem 105, and will continue with the same amount of hours since Chem 101 is the same as Chem 105/115. The Parachute Program has worked out well and I'm hopeful other cours-

Students get a jump start on their first Biology course by participating in Biology Bootcamp prior to the fall semester.

es on campus that could implement this strategy would choose to do so.

ACADEMIC SUPPORT

Identify your current academic support initiatives/program/courses designed to help freshmen succeed.

Who are the people and/or departments responsible for academic support?

_____

_____

_____

_____

What types of support do they provide?

_____

_____

_____

How does their involvement benefit freshman retention?

_____

_____

_____

Brainstorm ways to further explore academic support opportunities.

_____

_____

_____

_____

_____

_____

Interview

Dr. Rebekah Reysen

CSSFYE Assistant Director-Academic Support Programs

Describe your role in the University's retention efforts.

I am the Assistant Director of Academic Support Programs for the CSSFYE. I coordinate programs for academically at-risk undergraduates - those who have less than a 2.0 cumulative Grade Point Average. These courses include EDHE 101, Academic Skills for College; EDHE 202, Fundamentals of Active Learning; the Contractual Readmission Program; and EDHE 303, Academic Skills for Transfer Students. These programs serve well over 1,000 at-risk students each year. I also coordinate the UM Certified Peer Mentorship program, which involves training undergraduates to be positive role models on campus. Any department can request that their students be trained through the CSSFYE, so I have been actively training a variety of peer mentor groups since the program began several years ago. I also conduct academic consultations, where I meet with students and/or their parents to discuss optimal study habits, removing barriers to academic success, and developing academic success plans. Additionally, I enjoy conducting presentations on academic success strategies such as time management, test analyses, note taking, creating study guides, etc. for instructors who request in-class presentations.

Additionally, frequently conduct research projects on retention and student success, and on topics such as grit, motivation, self-efficacy, academic entitlement, and specific academic success strategies. I have published a variety of research articles and book chapters that focus on college student development, and I also like to present at conferences as often as possible. I like to get "the word out" about all of our great retention initiatives at Ole Miss! And I love pedagogy, so I teach a section of EDHE 105 for FASTrack every fall semester and a section of EDHE 101 in the spring.

In your opinion, what are some of the most effective retention strategies at the University?

I am so impressed by the work ethic that our student affairs professionals have and the amount of attention our leaders devote to helping students persist in their studies. I don't think our efforts would be nearly as effective without the support of our administration, as well as the energy that the staff channels each day into helping students. So the people of Ole Miss are what I think make it such a great institution. Everyone loves their job and playing a major role in helping students. Additionally, our data show that each one of our retention initiatives has been successful in its own right. I like how our administration encourages the coordinators of our EDHE courses to continually research the effectiveness of our programs, and our statistics show that those who engage in our programs are much more likely to persist in their studies than those who do not.

Since you became involved in the University's retention efforts, describe some changes you have observed.

I originally became involved in our retention efforts as a graduate student volunteer back in 2007, with the EDHE 202 program.

Since that time, I have noticed that all of our retention programs have grown significantly. EDHE 101 and 202 have grown substantially in the number of sections offered to students. EDHE 303 became an official course in the Spring of 2016 and is going to be expanded from its original sole section to potentially 13-15 sections in the Spring of 2017. Our mentorship program became an official program in 2012, and we have been certifying mentors since that time. The Contractual Readmission Program was also started in 2012 and has served hundreds of students since its' inception. Our non-at-risk programs, such as EDHE 105 and EDHE 305 have also grown as well.

Where do you see retention efforts going in the short term? Long term?

In the short-term I would say that we will keep trying to serve as many students as possible by providing academic consultations, mentorship opportunities, as well as the opportunity to participate in our EDHE programs. With the freshman class growing in size each year, we can anticipate more and more students needing assistance through our services. In the long-term I would like to see official classes being offered at the university for both undergraduates and graduate students looking to serve as peer mentors. I have recently put in a request to our administration to offer such courses, along with potentially offering for-credit minors for students (both graduates and undergraduates) looking to assist our academically at-risk and non-at-risk students. Offering these minors could help our mentors not only receive valuable course credit and opportunities to gain important professional skills that they could use in the work place; but they would also be a cost-effective solution for the university in that these mentors could assist students with providing free mentorship opportunities. It would be a win-win situation for the mentors, the mentees, and for our retention numbers. Dr. Wells-Dolan from the School of Education and I are collaborating on these initiatives and we look forward to seeing what the future may hold in these areas. I also anticipate collaborating with K-12 institutions to see what retention efforts they may be utilizing to prepare students to become effective learners at the collegiate level.

What advice would you give other institutions regarding their retention efforts?

I believe retention efforts are most successful when the administration and staff at the university are working in-tandem for the needs of the students. If staff are enthusiastic about helping students, then I think great things can happen and new initiatives can be created. What I also think is crucial is a positive work environment. At Ole Miss, everyone is a team and members of each department can communicate easily and frequently to assist with student development. So if an institution has that kind of work environment, then again, great things can happen.

I am also a strong believer in assessment and data analysis. I recommend institutions lean on the expertise of their statisticians, data analysts, and Institutional Research, Effectiveness, and Planning offices to explore which student groups need the most support. Are their certain demographic characteristics, such as financial, in-state/out-of-state, level of parent education, etc. that could point us in a particular direction of how certain student groups perform? What about students in specific majors? Do some perform better than others? Tailoring interventions to these specific groups could prove to be very beneficial for increasing student retention.

I recommend using a framework that we use here at UM with the EDHE 105/ 305, 101/303, 202, CRP, and FASTrack (to name a few) course, which have demonstrated the ability to influence retention numbers in a positive way. Last, but not least, we have a retention committee here at the University that is comprised of individuals from many different departments on campus. We are all very enthusiastic about student retention, and I would be happy to "talk shop" with anyone interested in this area!

INITIATIVE 12
SPECIAL COHORT PROGRAMS

The ability to group new students into special cohorts has many advantages. As most retention professionals will attest, helping freshmen get connected to campus is vital to retention efforts. Special cohorts are a way to assist freshmen connect to peers, faculty/staff associated with the cohorts, campus programs, and other facets of the institution. Additionally, students who are members of a special cohort will have a campus professional responsible for them. We consider this person to be a "special cohort owner," who not only plays a key role in supporting the members of the special cohort, but also is heavily relied on to ensure these specific students persist from year one to year two.

> Helping freshmen get connected to campus is vital to retention efforts.

There are two different classifications of special cohorts at the University of Mississippi. One classification is by program in which the student has opted to join, such as FASTrack, Honors College, etc. This category typically involves a smaller number of students and has more programming features as a way to proactively support students. The other type of special cohort is a broader category which the University has grouped freshmen together such as students enrolled in EDHE 105, minority freshmen, etc. Although students in these types of cohorts do have some programming, it is not as defined as the first cohort type. Additionally, interaction with members of this cohort classification is more reactive.

Many members of the Retention Advisory Board are considered special cohort owners.

Since freshman retention became a serious priority at the University of Mississippi in 2008, new special cohorts of freshmen have been created. Each of these new cohorts and all others that previously existed have a special cohort owner. Cohort owners of specific programs are expected to get to know new freshmen early in the semester, plan programming, and understand how their role as a cohort owner impacts freshman retention. They should be seen as a trusted campus professional who can help address any issue that a freshman may encounter at the University. Cohort owners who oversee a broad cohort (e.g., freshmen who owe a large balance, live on campus, etc.) are more reactive in their efforts. This group of owners must wait on data that could affect persistence then attempt to address the issue(s) with individual students.

Special cohort owners have many responsibilities when it comes to their students persisting. Regardless if a cohort owner oversees a special program or a broad category, she understands the nature of the position and when to act regarding persistence issues. Several examples of a cohort owner reacting to persistence data could include: no schedule, low midterms, holds, and academic standing. After priority registration has concluded for the upcoming semester, the Center for Student Success and First-Year Experience's (CSSFYE) Assistant Director-Retention creates a report including all freshman cohort members, who have yet to register for the upcoming semester. This report features much information, including any special cohorts of which the student may be a member. Each cohort owner receives an individual report of freshmen who fall under his/her area of oversight. I rely on these owners to make contact with freshmen on the list and to help them get registered or make notes in the retention tool, regarding persistence barriers or whether the student plans on returning to the University. Similar to no-schedule reports, cohort owners also receive a list of their freshmen with low mid-term grades. In smaller cohort programs (e.g., Luckyday, first-generation, etc.) the owner can reach out to individual freshmen on the list and offer assistance. However, for broad category cohorts (e.g., EDHE 105, minority students, etc.) the owner may create a mail-merge e-mail listing various academic resources on campus. Clearing all holds before priority registration begins ensures the student will get to register as soon as his/her registration window opens, thus offering a better chance to create an optimal schedule for academic success. Cohort owners are sent a list of their freshmen, who have holds one month prior to registration windows opening. Owners are able to remind students about the hold, how to clear the hold, and the importance of registering for classes as early as possible. Additionally, during the short time window when the Bursar removes the hold for freshmen who owe $400 or less, owners follow up with their freshmen to make sure they are taking advantage of the Bursar's opportunity. The final example of how cohort owners react to information is when freshmen in their cohort fall out of good academic standing. Cohort owners receive these lists at the conclusion of the fall and spring semesters. Owners have the opportunity to offer words of encouragement, explore issues that affected their academics, and inform about University policies as they relate to academic standing (e.g., EDHE 101 requirement, Contractual Readmission Program, etc.).

Many members of the Retention Advisory Board are considered special cohort owners. These campus professionals are extremely valuable in the University's retention efforts. Not only do they value helping our students be successful, they fully understand the mission of the Retention Advisory Board and how important their cohort work is regarding the big picture. Several members of the Board oversee programs that are considered special cohorts. Some examples include: Assistant Dean of

Liberal Arts –FASTrack, Director of Luckyday–Luckyday Program, and the Assistant Director-Academic Support Programs for the Center for Student Success and First-Year Experience–Contractual Readmission Program. Other Board members have oversight of broad category special cohorts. Examples of these owners include: Associate Director Center for Student Success and First-Year Experience—EDHE 105 course, Director of the Center for Inclusion and Cross Cultural Engagement—Minority freshmen, and the Assistant Director of Student Housing—Freshmen living in residence halls. Each of these individuals contribute to the overall work of the Board, but also focus their attention on individual freshmen who fall under their special cohort.

Special Cohorts at the University of Mississippi

The University of Mississippi has a wide array of special cohorts on campus. As previously mentioned, one retention strategy we utilize is to create broad categories in which freshmen may fall under and designate a cohort owner for that particular group. This type of cohort is usually large there are not many (if any) specific programming options or much proactive outreach. Therefore, for the remainder of this initiative I am going to focus on several of our special cohort programs that offer defined programming, outreach, and support.

FASTrack

FASTtrack is a special cohort program for new freshmen at the University who opt to participate. FASTrack stands for Foundations of Academic Success Track and is coordinated through the College of Liberal Arts. An assistant dean, with the help of several staff members, oversees the program. Most new freshmen are welcome to apply to the program. In my opinion, FASTrack helps make the campus feel smaller and as-

FASTrack students get to know each other by participating in team-building activities at the Ole Miss Ropes Course.

sists students in making connections within their learning community. There are many advantages to participating in FASTrack. Program participants take three classes that count toward most majors (e.g., EDHE 105, WRIT 101, PSY 201, etc.) each semester during their freshman year. Students can choose their other two courses, similar to other freshmen, and FASTrack freshmen are encouraged to enroll in 15-16 hours each semester. The instructors for FASTrack-only sections are carefully selected, to ensure these students will have a great experience in the classroom. FASTrack students have their own academic advisor who is employed by the program. Additionally, participants are supported by academic and peer mentors. Academic mentors are campus professionals who can help new freshmen with any transition that may arise, as well as offer academic assistance. The peer mentors are other undergraduates who can help participants navigate the first year of college. FASTrack students can live together in a newer residence hall on campus. Although living within the learning community is not required, it is highly recommended. Students interested in FASTrack apply before they arrive for summer orientation. Space is limited and there is a one-time $400 program fee. FASTrack plans to have 400 participants from the 2016 freshman cohort. From a retention perspective, I appreciate the good work that comes from the FASTrack program. These freshmen have good retention rates, and their staff is fully committed to our retention efforts.

Honors College

The Sally McDonnell Barksdale Honors College at the University of Mississippi is unique in that we consider it a special cohort program, but it is also recognized as an academic college. Many of the new freshmen with the highest entering academic metrics are members of the Honors College. The Honors College has 350 freshmen who averaged 30 on the ACT. Similar to FASTrack, the Honors College does a good job of helping their freshmen acclimate to college life. There is no cost to be in the Honors College, but it does require a very competitive application process. Additionally, students who are not accepted as freshmen, can reapply to enter the Honors College as a junior. Honors College freshmen are required to take HON 101 during

Tom Brokow speaks to a group of Honors College students

the fall semester and HON 102 during the spring semester. Other courses that may be required for a student's major, (BISC 160, CHEM 105, MATH 261, etc.) will have honors-only sections. Students are not required to take specific honors-only sections, but must accumulate enough hours of honors credit as they persist toward their degree. Honors-only sections of courses are usually smaller than sections for traditional students and are taught by faculty selected by the Honors College. Freshmen in the Honors College may choose to live in the Honors Living and Learning Community, but this is not a requirement. The Honors College has its own building and allows members 24-hour access. Additionally, Honors College members have an honors advisor who, in conjunction with their assigned academic advisor, supports them during the first year and beyond. Honors College freshmen have the highest retention rates of all special cohorts. On the rare occasion an Honors College freshman does not persist, Honors College staff are already aware of the issue(s) and work with other University representatives as they relate to retention.

Provost Scholars

The Provost Scholars program was created in 2010 as a way to encourage high academic achieving freshmen who did not get accepted into the Honors College to still enroll at the University of Mississippi. Today the program has evolved into a special cohort that has many advantages for participants. Although some students who did not get into the Honors College will opt to apply as Provost Scholars, other participants may not have had any interest in the Honors College and chose the Provost Scholars program based solely on merits of the program. Provost Scholars continues to increase membership every year. In 2014 there were over 700 freshmen who participated in Provost Scholars. Those students had an ACT average of 28. The Provost Scholars program is coordinated out of the Office of the Provost. One benefit of being in this free program is early registration. Provost Scholars are allowed to register before their peers who have a similar number of earned hours. Provost Scholars are invited to attend a special seminar before the beginning of their fall semester. Additionally, they have opportunities to meet and mingle with staff members from the Office of the Provost, deans and faculty members. Other programming opportunities are offered during the academic year. Although Provost Scholars have good entering academic metrics, this is one group I feel should be retained at a higher level. Unfortunately, we do lose some Provost Scholar freshmen each year. Reasons given for a lack of persistence vary. We hear of students leaving for financial concerns (these freshmen do not receive as much scholarship money as some other groups on campus), admitted to first choice institution as transfer students, and other reasons. I am hopeful the Provost Scholar program will continue to explore ways to help their freshmen persist.

Luckyday

The Luckyday program is a smaller cohort program that is very successful in helping their freshmen get acclimated to college life. Each fall semester the Luckyday program accepts 75 new freshmen. These students are awarded some scholarship money and live in the Luckyday Residential College (LRC). This is the only special cohort to have an entire residence hall dedicated to one program. In my opinion, the LRC is a tremendous asset to this program's success. Luckyday students in the LRC live in one of the newer residence halls on campus. This residence hall has its own dining hall, study rooms, and computer lab. Therefore, Luckyday freshmen have

Luckyday students have the opportunity to live in their own residential college.

numerous opportunities to have natural interaction, thus forming a small community, which is connected to the institution. The Luckyday program provides a variety of services to their freshmen. Luckyday freshmen participate in a retreat prior to the beginning of the fall semester. The retreat affords students the opportunity to get to know each other, participate in team-building activities, and learn about the University. Once students officially begin the fall semester, they are invited to listen to speakers and attend various Luckyday programs that can be educational, social, or service learning in nature. Additionally, a Luckyday initiative that I believe serves program participants well is their peer mentoring program. New freshmen are paired with upperclassmen peer mentors who also are part of the Luckyday program. The mentor/mentee relationship is another resource for freshmen as they transition from high school to college student. The cohort owner of this group is on the Retention Advisory Board. He is very active in retention efforts for this special cohort program. Luckyday freshmen are retained at higher levels than the overall freshman cohort.

StudentsFIRST

Most institutions understand the struggles that many first-generation college students encounter during their initial year of college. The University of Mississippi created StudentsFIRST as a support program for first-generation students. The "FIRST" in StudentsFIRST stands for Freshmen Interactively Reaching Success Together. StudentsFIRST is a very worthwhile support program for first-generation students. Unfortunately, it is difficult to get first-generation students to participate in the program. First-generation freshmen are identified early in the summer so the StudentsFIRST coordinator can make contact with the student/family prior to their arrival for summer orientation. The program coordinator works with the Office of Admissions and Financial Aid to identify potential first-generation freshmen. Unfortunately, the data is not always accurate, as it is optional for students to list their parents' highest level of education on the admissions application. First-generation freshmen who choose to participate in the program are offered various forms of support. Peer mentoring is one initiative that has been hit or miss. During some years there are very good mentors who attend training, are ready to assist other first-generation students, and a good mentor/mentee relationship is formed. However, there have been other years where it was difficult to identify upperclassmen to serve as peer mentors or new freshmen were not interested in having a mentor. In addition to mentoring, the StudentsFIRST coordinator provides educational and social programs for first-generation freshmen. Attendance at these programs is usually higher early in the semester when students are still trying to find their niche. Unfortunately, attendance declines later in the year, as students have made other connections or do not believe they need the information being presented at the program. From my observations the most powerful component of this program is the fact that the coordinator is a first-generation student and truly cares about this population's success. Although peer mentoring or program participation may not be ideal, many of these students meet individually on a regular basis with the program coordinator. They see her as a trusted agent at the University. Her door is always open for them to seek assistance. Because the coordinator introduces herself early in the students' academic careers, the potential for relationships to develop is a significant benefit to this program.

Student Veterans

Student veterans are an important group to retain and keep on track to a timely graduation. This special population has a specific amount of time in which to earn degrees once they begin using their Veterans Administration (VA) benefits. The cohort owner for this special cohort program at the University of Mississippi is the Coordinator of Veterans and Military Services. This person performs a variety of proactive and reactive functions in order to help this special cohort be successful. The coordinator identifies new student veterans when they enter the University through their admission application. Once the student is admitted, the coordinator begins communication. He gives a presentation at orientation and invites all new student veterans to come to his office while on campus for orientation so they can get to know each other while he informs them on the VA paperwork process. During the semester he welcomes student veterans to contact him with any academic or non-academic issue that may arise. Additionally, he schedules programs, sends out important information, and advises the Student Veterans of America chapter on campus. This cohort owner must also be reactive when he receives information about students in his special cohort who are in need of support. No matter if he is notified of students with low mid-term grades or those who have not registered for the upcoming semester, his willingness to help is easily identified. The Coordinator of Veterans and Military Services also is a veteran, thus his ability to relate to our student veterans is an asset to the University's support and retention of this special population.

Housing's Living and Learning Communities

The recognition of Living and Learning Communities (LLC) across the country continues to be a popular trend regarding supporting and retaining students. It would seem obvious this would be a hot topic among Student Housing, but I am seeing, reading, and hearing about LLCs in the context of academic advising, retention, first-year experience, and other areas of higher education. LLCs at the University of Mississippi are relatively new, but gaining in popularity. Additionally, the University utilizes Living Groups (LG) as a way for students with similar interests to live together. For the 2016-17 academic year, there are only three LLCs: Early Entry Pharmacy, FASTrack, and Honors College. However, there are eight LGs with four being for freshmen only. The freshmen only LG include: Provost Scholars, Leadership, STEM, and Red, Blue & Green. Living and Learning Communities and Learning Groups have many shared characteristics. They both strive to help new freshmen establish a sense of community with other new peers who have similar interests. Faculty/staff involvement, programs, and other features are highlights of these special cohorts. The primary differences among the LLCs are directly related to an academic major, program, or college on campus. Whereas, LGs are loosely tailored by a common interest, such as students who want to enhance their leadership skills (Leadership) or those who value the environment and sustainability of the University. Each community/group has a faculty or staff member who oversees the program. Additionally, the Housing Department representative on the Retention Advisory Board is able to serve as the cohort owner for all freshmen in residence halls, which includes those participating in LLC and LG. Attracting and keeping students engaged and connected to the institution is extremely important in retention efforts. I believe that Housing is assisting us in these key facets of retention through their efforts with LLC and LG. I am hopeful this initiative will continue to expand and more new freshmen will take advantage of this wonderful opportunity.

SPECIAL COHORT PROGRAMS

Does your institution currently group freshmen together by special cohorts?

Who are the people and/or departments responsible for current cohorts?

_____

_____

_____

_____

What types of support do they provide?

_____

_____

_____

How does their involvement benefit freshman retention?

_____

_____

_____

Brainstorm ways to create and/or expand special cohort programs for freshmen.

_____

_____

_____

_____

_____

_____

Interview

Dr. Stephen Monroe

Assistant Dean of the College of Liberal Arts and Director of FASTrack

Describe your role in the University's retention efforts.

I am co-chair (with the author of this book) of UM's Retention Advisory Board. I direct FASTrack, a learning community program that serves more than 400 students, some 10% of the first-year class. Over the years, I've contributed in whatever way possible to increasing student access and success. We have a tradition at UM of supporting students. Many of us are devoted to continuing that tradition and to making it even stronger in the coming years. We proudly serve students from all backgrounds. Students come to UM with various levels of preparation, and we want them all to learn and succeed. We are an elite R1 university; we are also an open-access university for the students of Mississippi. This complicated identity creates challenges, of course, but it is also highly motivating. We see student opportunities turn into student successes every day.

In your opinion, what are some of the most effective retention strategies at the University?

Students are more likely to succeed when they feel welcomed and supported. College is challenging academically and socially. Our most successful strategies address the whole student. FASTrack works well because it is multi-layered and personal. We build real relationships with our students through smaller classes and personalized mentoring. We make early connections before problems develop. Then, when students need help during a difficult time, they are talking to friends and allies, not to strangers.

Since you became involved in the University's retention efforts, describe some changes you have observed.

We do a wonderful job of coordinating our work and of avoiding territorialism. On some campuses, student affairs and academic affairs are siloed and sometimes even at odds. Here, we all work together. We may have different perspectives and even different approaches to helping students. Even then, though, we know that we share a common mission. The result is that student success has not become an isolated purpose. No one office or division "owns" the mission of helping students. We are all invested in the work and thus much more likely to succeed. Partnerships and communication across division lines are not always easy to maintain, but they are absolutely vital.

Where do you see retention efforts going in the short term? Long term?

I now consider our program to be mature. We have years of practice and data, and we've learned carefully from our mistakes and successes. We're not doing any one revolutionary thing. All of our "interventions" can be found on their own at other institutions. What we've done, though, is created our own proprietary blend of practices, to create a learning community model that works very well for our particular students. In the coming years, we will refine that blend and expand our scale. I would like for every first-year student at UM to be in a learning community.

What advice would you give other institutions regarding their retention efforts?

It's important for leaders at all levels to talk about student success. We've benefited from a provost and chancellor who have set the right tone and who have been consistent over the years. This has empowered those of us in the classrooms and offices to make this work an ongoing priority.

Also, I believe strongly that vocabulary is very important. It is dangerous to reduce this work to a single metric. If we only talk about "retention rate," for example, we are losing sight of the larger mission. We are in education to help students learn about the world and about themselves. We don't simply want to retain them on campus. Retention, in and of itself, is not an end goal. I try to remind myself of this difference every day because it influences how I view and interact with my students. They must come first, ahead even of our worthy institutional goals.

INITIATIVE 13
CONTACTING STUDENTS

Working with students to address individual persistence issues should be at the core of all successful retention programs. One of the best ways to uncover potential or current persistence barriers is through direct student contact. When campus professionals contact students, they open the door for students to work with someone affiliated with the institution to address a specific issue. Communication may be in broad form such as a generic mass e-mail, or targeted to an individual student via phone call regarding that student's specific information. Furthermore, communication to students can be both proactive and reactive. This initiative will explore various proactive and reactive forms of communication that are utilized with University of Mississippi freshmen.

One of the best ways to uncover potential or current persistence barriers is through direct student contact.

Proactive Forms of Communication

Welcome letter and e-mail from academic advisor

During the summer, after incoming freshmen have attended Summer Orientation, academic advisors in the Center for Student Success and First-Year Experience send new advisees a welcome letter to the student's home address and an e-mail to the student's official University e-mail account. Advisors provide the students information about themselves, the

---

Hello <Student>!

I hope you had a wonderful experience at Freshman Orientation and are excited to begin your academic journey at The University of Mississippi. My name is *Academic Advisor Name*. I am your Academic Advisor in the Center for Student Success and First-Year Experience (CSSFYE). As a freshman in the *Name of School/College* you will be assigned a professional academic advisor in the CSSFYE to assist you with all your needs as a new student. I will assist you with class registration, department curricula, university policies, and other academic facets. Additionally, I will be happy to help you with any non-academic issues/questions that may arise during your first year.

You WILL be required to meet with me in the fall and spring to have your Advisor Hold removed. However, you are welcome to contact me as often as needed.

If you have any questions before your arrival or once you are here please feel free to contact me. I look forward to having you at Ole Miss.

Important Dates –
Fall semester begins on August 22
Advising begins September 12 for Spring and Winter Intersession 2017
Registration begins October 24 for Spring and Winter Intersession 2017
Thanksgiving Break will be November 21-25
Final exam week will be December 5-9

Best,

Academic Advisor Name
Academic Advisor Contact Information

Center for Student Success and First-Year Experience (CSSFYE), as well as open the door for students to ask advisors questions before the start of the fall semester. This approach has worked out well in providing information earlier to new students and decreased the number of questions students may have after they have already arrived on campus. Furthermore, many new freshmen ask advisors questions prior to their arrival on campus. It is not uncommon for students to have questions about their schedules, transfer work, AP credit, or other issues related to being a new student. Although this proactive outreach costs money in postage, letterhead, and envelopes, I believe the benefits outweigh the costs, as students can have questions addressed earlier and an established point of contact before they arrive for classes in August.

Academic advisor e-mail during the first week of the semester

During the first week of the fall semester CSSFYE academic advisors send an e-mail to all new freshman advisees' official University account and their alternative e-mail address (in case students have not began checking their University account). For many of the new students, the e-mail is a re-introduction since the advisors sent communication to them over the summer. For other students who attended the final orientation session in August, or changed their major over the summer, the e-mail is their first opportunity to meet their assigned academic advisor. Regardless of which group a student falls under, every student is given advisors' contact information, told of important items to consider during the first of the semester, and encouraged to contact advisors with questions or concerns. Once the e-mail is sent, students begin to contact their advisors via e-mail, phone, and office visits. The most common issue during the first week is the student's desire to adjust her schedule. The e-mail is usually sent mid-week, so most students have had the opportunity to attend every class at least once. Some students may realize they are in the wrong class, ill-prepared for the content, or disapproving of the time the class meets. The ability to discuss other class options with their advisors and make changes on the spot provides comfort to many concerned students. Additionally, the student has now formed an introductory relationship with his academic advisor and hopefully, feels confident in contacting the advisor with any future concerns.

Enrolling in EDHE 105

As previously discussed in other initiatives, I am a firm believer in the support that our EDHE 105 course, "The Freshman Year Experience," provides new freshmen. At the conclusion of summer orientations, the CSSFYE assistant director-retention creates a report to identify new freshmen who chose not to enroll in EDHE 105 and who are considered at-risk. For this initiative, we consider "at-risk" new freshmen who have majors of undeclared or business undeclared, have an ACT score below 22, and/or a high school GPA below a 3.0. The assistant director-retention sends each CSSFYE academic advisor a list of students who fall in the aforementioned categories. The advisors then contact the students and encourage them to enroll in EDHE 105 for the fall semester. Any new freshman who falls under the at-risk categories, but does not have a professional advisor, is contacted by the assistant director-retention. Many students who are contacted choose to enroll in the course after learning about the benefits from University staff members. The other type of contact we make with new freshmen regarding EDHE 105 is for those freshmen who attend the final orientation session in August. The University has years of data that indicate freshmen who attend August Orientation enter with lower academic metrics, earn lower first year GPAs, and persist at lower levels than their peers who attended earlier orientation sessions. Therefore, in 2012 the Academic Support Center (now the Center for Student Success and First-Year Experience) began enrolling all August Orientation attendees in EDHE 105 before they arrived on campus. These students were informed about enrollment and

Hello 2016 freshmen not currently registered for EDHE 105,

Because not all new freshmen are checking their official Ole Miss email account, I am sending this note to all email addresses associated with your account.

I hope this email finds you doing well. Now that you have attended most of your classes, you should have a good idea of the academic demands and initial expectations of your performance for each course. With that said, it is not too late to add our EDHE 105 "Freshman Year Experience" course to your schedule.

Although this course is optional, it is highly recommended for new freshmen. Please remember that EDHE 105:

- is worth 3-credit hours
- is letter-graded
- counts the same as every other course on our campus (e.g. Biology, Calculus, etc.)
- is applicable to almost all degree programs
- is only offered during the fall of your freshman year
- is all about helping you make the successful transition from high school to college
- is one of the smallest classes you will take (around 24 freshmen per section)
- has the most sections on campus (128 sections offered this fall)
- enrolls almost 80% of the freshman class
- covers topics such as: time management, college study strategies, campus resources, and other topics designed to assist first-year freshmen
- has supplementary components that are specifically designed to help new freshmen such as: personality/interest assessment, Career Center tour/presentations, and other guest speakers/outside of class activities.

http://cssfye.olemiss.edu/first-year-experience/edhe-105/

Each fall semester numerous new freshmen and their parents contact me about enrolling in EDHE 105 after the last day to add a course (this fall that day is September 2). This panic email, phone call, or office visit usually occurs due to the student making a poor grade on a test, paper, etc. in a different course, realizing college courses are more demanding than high school courses, and/or receiving their mid-term grades. Unfortunately, once these issues occur it is too late for students to add EDHE 105.

If you are interested in adding EDHE 105 to your schedule, you can do so online in your myOleMiss account through this Friday, August 26. If you decide you would like to add next week, you must come to 350 Martindale to be added. At the conclusion of the second week (September 2), students are no longer able to add courses. You can drop a course through October 3 via your myOleMiss account.

Please let me know if you have any questions.

Kyle Ellis, Ph.D.
Director, Center for Student Success and First-Year Experience

given information about the course via e-mail and letters to their home address. Additionally, the students were told they could drop the course or change sections, if needed. At Orientation, these new freshmen and their parents are reminded about the course and encouraged to remain enrolled. Most remain in the section in which they were manually enrolled once they see that course selection is very limited three days before the semester begins.

Question:

How important is early outreach to new freshmen at your institution?

Invitations

The goal of getting new freshmen connected to an institution is a priority for campus professionals who work in retention. At the University of Mississippi, we plan numerous programs and have policies in place where students have the opportunity to get connected. Unfortunately, some new freshmen who could benefit the most do not take advantage of the opportunities that are afforded to them. In an effort to assist freshmen in getting connected, staff members from the CSSFYE contact students and invite them to participate in various events. In the past the CSSFYE sponsored a campus-wide major fair, where all academic departments were represented in one convenient location for students to learn about all majors at the University. Though the event was open to any student, our target audience was comprised of undeclared students. Advisors would contact all undeclared students and encourage them to attend. Furthermore, the e-mail would invite the student to come and introduce him/herself to the advisor at the CSSFYE table. A recent initiative encouraged CSSFYE staff members to invite new freshmen to attend our the regional/state meet-and-greets. During the first three weeks of the semester the CSSFYE hosts several meet-and-greets for new freshmen. These meetings are organized by geographic region or state. The goal is to target new freshmen who are far from home. Some states such as Florida and Illinois have over 100 residents in the freshman cohort, so they have their own state meet-and-greet. However, other states that are farther away such as California, Arizona, and Oregon need to be grouped together to form a West Coast meet-and-greet. CSSFYE staff members send students from these states personal e-mails inviting them to attend the freshman event that corresponds to their region/state. Parents from these areas also are informed of the events and are asked to encourage their freshmen to attend.

Some invitations that are sent align with University policy. For example, every student at the University is required to meet with an academic advisor before they are allowed to register for the upcoming semester. CSSFYE Academic Advisors begin contacting their advisees early in the semester and inviting them to come in for advising sessions. This proactive outreach allows the student to meet before the registration rush and have more one-on-one time with the academic advisor. Additionally, this invitation serves as another reminder of the student's academic advisor's contact information and the advisor's willingness to help the student with any issue he/she may be experiencing. The early outreach also allows advisors to spread their advising appointments out over the semester so they are not overloaded when registration open later in the semester. If students have not been in to see their advisor after all registration windows have opened, advisors will continue contact efforts. Other policy-related communication with students may come from Financial Aid, Housing, or student groups.

Hello New Freshmen from Illinois,

I hope this email finds you doing well and your semester is off to a good start. I would like to invite all new Ole Miss freshmen from Illinois to attend our Illinois Freshman Meet and Greet. The event will be held Thursday, September 10, 2015 in the Bondurant Auditorium (http://map.olemiss.edu/?id=11257270) at 5:00 p.m. The primary purpose of this event is for you to meet other new Ole Miss freshmen from your state. The event will last about an hour and will include light refreshments. We are hopeful that following the event, attendees will go to dinner together and continue their conversations. I strongly encourage you to take advantage of this special event. No RSVP required.

Illinois

- **Thursday Sept. 10, 2015** in the Bondurant Auditorium at 5:00pm

- CSSFYE Hosts:

THIS EMAIL WAS SENT TO ILLINOIS FRESHMAN STUDENTS' OLE MISS EMAIL, STUDENTS' ALT EMAIL, AND PARENTS/GUARDIANS' EMAILS WE HAVE ON FILE.

Transition Survey

The Office of Institutional Research Effectiveness and Planning (IREP) at the University of Mississippi sends all new students an online transition survey. The survey is sent during the third week of the semester. The survey focuses on students' initial expectations, as well as how they are adjusting to the University. At the end of the survey students have the opportunity to offer additional thoughts. Additionally, they can request that a campus professional follow up with them regarding any issue. When IREP learns that a student has requested follow up, they send the request to the CSSFYE's assistant director-retention. This person reads the student's comments, contacts him directly and either asks the student's academic advisor to make contact, or sends the request to the appropriate person on campus, who may be in another department (e.g., Financial Aid, Parking Services, etc.). IREP's proactive approach in allowing new students the opportunity to express questions or concerns early in the semester, has assisted the University in ensuring that these students have a good experience during their first semester.

Summer classes and Contractual Readmission Program

At the conclusion of the spring semester, I am hopeful our freshman retention rate is extremely high, as I know we will experience a "summer melt" during the months of June and July. The summer melt is when freshmen, who have fall semester schedules, choose to drop their courses. These students, who have not been on our retention radar because they had a fall schedule, thus were considered retained. One group that is prone to drop their fall schedule over the summer is composed of students who did not do well academically during their first year. A strategy we have implemented to slow the melt for this population is to contact freshmen who are placed on academic suspension, and who are enrolled in summer courses at the University. Every situation is different based on the student's GPA, number of hours enrolled, ability to use forgiveness grades, etc. However, the overarching theme is to guide students in getting off academic suspension and/or encouraging them to consider the Contractual Readmission Program. If students who are placed on academic suspension after the fall semester choose to enroll in 12 credit hours in an attempt to get back in good standing, but do not earn a 2.0 in those summer courses, they will be placed on academic dismissal. Therefore, we would not be able to retain them with the Contractual Readmission Program. Advisors must monitor their progress during summer courses to ensure they stop taking classes once they have returned to good standing, or are close to being placed on academic dismissal. Each year we have a small number of freshmen who disregard our advice and take 12 hours over the summer only to earn less than a 2.0 and move from academic suspension to academic dismissal. Monitoring summer course work for academically suspended freshmen and encouraging participation in the Contractual Readmission Program has helped us slow the melt.

Reactive Forms of Communication

Students with holds

During other initiatives outlined in this book, I noted the importance of students registering for courses as soon as their registration windows opened. Because campus professionals who value retention understand this important component, numerous staff members are involved in contacting freshmen who have holds before registration for the upcoming semester. Any hold on a student's account will prevent course registration for the upcoming semester. Therefore, it is imperative that students clear all holds before their registration windows open. Several weeks before students can register, the Center for Student Success and First-Year Experience (CSSFYE) assistant director-retention creates and distributes holds reports to owners of holds. These reports only contain information for freshmen. They include the type of hold (e.g., Bursar, Student Conduct, etc.) on the student's account and contact information. Holds owners are then asked to contact all freshmen on the report and assist them in removing the hold. Based on our experience with this initiative, the number of holds steadily decreases as the CSSFYE continues to send weekly hold reports until registration windows open.

Low mid-term grades

I am hopeful that each and every freshman who begins at the University of Mississippi is successful academically during his first year. Unfortunately, this is not always the case; after each fall semester some 10% (around 400) of the freshman cohort are placed on academic probation (having less than a 2.0 GPA). Identifying students who are struggling academically is a priority. After mid-term grades are reported, academic advisors, EDHE 101/105 instructors, and special cohort owners are notified of their freshmen who had low mid-term grades. We define low mid-term grades as two or more "D" or "F" grades. The CSSFYE's assistant director-retention coordinates this initiative. Staff members who receive a list of their freshmen also receive instructions on how to assist the struggling students. The staff members are asked to contact each student. The goal is to assist students in creating a success plan for the remainder of the semester and utilizing the appropriate campus resources for the courses with low grades (e.g., writing course – Writing Center, math course – Math Lab, etc.). Some of the conversations occur via e-mail and telephone. However, I believe the most beneficial interventions occur during face-to-face meetings. Fortunately, this time period corresponds with academic advising for the upcoming semester, so many of the struggling freshmen have yet to see their academic advisors. The information on the report gives the advisors another reason to contact the students and encourages them to come in for advising. Utilizing the EDHE 105 instructors has been very beneficial as these campus professionals see the students several times a week in class. They are encouraged to have private meetings with struggling students. Although, the current practice of offering support based on mid-term grades works well, I would like to see a system where we could identify struggling freshmen earlier in the semester.

No-schedule

Course registration for the upcoming semester is the key metric used in our daily retention data. After all, course registration windows have opened for the next semester, the CSSFYE's assistant director-retention creates and distributes lists of freshmen without a schedule. Similar to low mid-grade reports, academic advisors, EDHE 101/105 instructors, and special cohort owners receive lists. Campus professionals are asked to contact individual freshmen on their lists and offer assistance with course registration. Some reasons for a lack of registration are easy to address, such as the student thought she did register, but instead had only saved courses as her "favorites." However, other issues are more cumbersome, such as the student may have a large financial balance. The front-line campus professionals do a good job of offering the students as much assistance as possible. When barriers to register are too much for the front-line professional to address, he will refer the student to other, specific staff members who can offer assistance. Of course the primary objective of this communication effort is to assist the student in registering for classes, but there are other benefits from this initiative. If a student informs the front line campus professional that he/she is not planning to return to the University, the staff member can obtain additional information and update the online retention tool. Occasionally, when campus administrators read the retention notes, extra assistance may be offered such as financial, social, academic, etc. Additionally, with staff members having a reason to contact freshmen on their lists, it opens the door for the students to discuss other current and/or potential issues. Although retention is the primary driving force for the initial contact, documenting reasons for departure and assisting the students with other aspects are positive alternate outcomes from this initiative.

Missing class

Initiative 9 highlighted the Freshman Attendance Based Initiative (FABI) that is utilized to support freshmen with multiple absences in a course during weeks 3-11 of a semester. After attendance is manually reported by the instructor or automatically uploaded to the FABI interface through the scanners in the classrooms, the CSSFYE assistant director-retention employs the program's communication model. The communication model relies on multiple people from several offices across campus. After a student misses three times in one course, he receives a generic e-mail from the CSSFYE assistant director-retention. The e-mail addresses the importance of class attendance, lists campus resources, and encourages the student to contact the staff member with any concerns. Additionally, a representative from Student Housing receives notification. This person divides the report by residence halls. Community assistants in each residence hall contact each student (usually via room visits)

Question:

Do you believe proactive or reactive outreach has a greater impact on retention? Why?

to discuss the importance of going to class and utilizing available campus resources. After the fourth absence in a course, in addition to the contacts above, the student's academic advisor and assistant dean of his school receive notification and are asked to follow up. If applicable, Athletics and Greek Life are sent the attendance information. If the student misses class a fifth time, all aforementioned contact efforts are made and the CSSFYE assistant director-retention calls the student. The goal of the phone call is to get the student to come in for a meeting. Finally, with six or more absences in a single class, a letter is sent to the student's home address and the Dean of Students is notified, in addition to all other contact efforts. Contacting students regarding class attendance can be time consuming for some staff members, but making students aware of the importance of going to class and the resources that are available to them, is a valued service in our retention efforts.

Temporary Bursar Hold removal

Each fall and spring semester for the last several years, the Bursar has been kind enough to temporarily remove their hold for freshmen who owe $400 or less after all registration windows have opened. This usually occurs around November 16 in the fall and April 16 in the spring. The holds will stay off until the Tuesday of final exam week. This ensures students are unable to receive a transcript of final grades without paying their balance. Because there is only a two- to three-week window of opportunity, CSSFYE academic advisors act swiftly in contacting freshmen. Fall semester has an added challenge, as one week of hold removal falls during the University's week-long Thanksgiving Break. When advisors contact freshmen on the list, they explain the urgency of registering as soon as possible due to the hold being reactivated. Advisors also encourage students to return in for additional assistance if some courses have closed, the student has changed her major, or for other issues that could affect course registration. Additionally, the CSSFYE's assistant director-retention creates a report of all freshmen who do not have a schedule and owe between $401-$1,000. Advisors receive this list and are asked to contact students who may be able to get their balance below $400 and take advantage of the Bursar's generosity. Each fall and spring semester we see a significant number of freshmen register thanks to the temporary hold removal and the advisors' contact attempts.

Good grades

Most of our communication with students involves reacting to an issue or attempting to be proactive in an effort to help a student avoid a potential problem. One form of communication that is reactive, but in a good way, is when CSSFYE academic advisors send freshmen, who earned good grades, a congratulatory note at the end of the semester. The notes are sent via e-mail and are simple and brief. They have two primary functions: to congratulate students on a job well done in the classroom, and to remind them that they are welcome to contact their advisor with any questions during the winter (if sent after fall semester) or summer (if sent after the spring semester) breaks. As previously stated, I place tremendous value on the advisors forming an effective and trustworthy relationship with their advisees. Communicating solely with advisees who have problems can wear down the advisor and cause the advisee to become unresponsive to the advisor's communication. By contacting students who do well, it is not uncommon for advisors to receive positive feedback and gratitude from their advisees, who did well academically.

Contacting freshmen using both proactive and reactive outreach has been beneficial in our retention efforts. Many of the contacts are made by front-line campus professionals who can offer assistance with a variety of issues. In my opinion, if campus professionals who are involved in retention efforts sit back and wait on freshmen to initiate contact after an issue has occurred, it may be too late and the student could potentially be lost.

Contacting Students

Identify your current methods for contacting freshmen.
Who are the people responsible for contact efforts?

_____

_____

_____

What types of contact is made?

_____

_____

_____

How do their contact efforts benefit freshman retention?

_____

_____

_____

Brainstorm ways to increase contact between freshmen and campus professionals.

_____

_____

_____

_____

_____

_____

INTERVIEW

Mariana Rangel
CSSFYE Academic Advisor and First-Year Experience Instructor

Describe your role in the University's retention efforts.

As an academic advisor at the Center for Student Success and First-Year Experience, I am assigned approximately 350 freshmen a year in a variety of majors. While helping students select classes, navigate course registration, and stay on track with their degree is a major part of my job, my role is certainly not limited to just that. Advisors in our office play a major role in freshman retention. We actively monitor information such as student absences, course performance, account holds that could prevent registration, and are in frequent contact with our students. In addition, we welcome questions and concerns from parents, as we believe their support plays an important role in retention. Towards the end of every semester, we maintain a list of freshmen who do not have schedules for the following semesters and work, while collaborating with other offices at the University, to help them remove barriers that prevent registration. Finally, I am responsible for teaching many sections of our Freshman Year and Transfer Year Experience courses. This course helps students adapt to all aspects of University life and is an important piece in the retention puzzle.

In your opinion, what are some of the most effective retention strategies at the University?

I truly believe in the value of a centralized advising system and the use of professional advisors, especially with our freshman students. Freshmen need much more attention than upperclassmen, as they learn to navigate college life. Having one-on-one advising that is easily accessible at all times in the semester is comforting to students, and allows advisors to become part of students' support systems. In addition, gathering data on the reasons why students leave the University through the Freshman Retention Tool has been tremendously valuable. Every time students drop their schedule, they are contacted by an academic advisor in the office who then updates the tool. Having access to this data has given us important insight and allowed us to make educated decisions about new initiatives.

Since you became involved in the University's retention efforts, describe some changes you have observed.

When it comes to retention, numbers are important and closely watched. I believe this has increased accountability within our office and has made us approach our job with a retention mindset. We are constantly brainstorming initiatives we believe could increase student persistence.

Where do you see retention efforts going in the short term? Long term?

The focus on retention is here to stay. Short term, we hope that our efforts and initiatives help increase our retention numbers and the success of our students. Long-term, I can see more advising and retention-related positions being created, the advisor-advisee ratio decreasing so that advisors can dedicate even more attention to their students, and more funding being allocated to retention initiatives. I also think we will increase our focus on the retention of transfer students, a population that is sometimes forgotten at many institutions.

What advice would you give other institutions regarding their retention efforts?

Having an office that is responsible for freshman retention is advantageous, but it is important to remember that retention is an University-wide effort. We have been fortunate at our University to rely on a number of constituencies such as the Office of Financial Aid, the Office of the Bursar, Student Housing, faculty, and others to help us with many initiatives. The creation of a Freshman Retention Tool has also helped us maintain retention-related information on our freshmen and utilize that data to help us improve our services.

INITIATIVE 14
CONNECTING STUDENTS TO EACH OTHER

If you have not gathered that I tremendously value connections as part of successful retention efforts, then please allow me to reiterate: GETTING STUDENTS CONNECTED IS ESSENTIAL TO A SUCCESSFUL RETENTION PROGRAM! Connections can be to a major, a faculty member, a staff member, an administrator, a special program, and peers, among others. Freshmen who are able to make more than one connection are likely to be successful, satisfied and persist at the institution. It is not uncommon for students who leave the University to mention that they never got connected to campus. Even students who cite such reasons for leaving as "wanting to be closer to home" or "transferring to an instate school" could have potentially been retained if they were connected to some aspect of the University and that connection outweighed their primary reason for leaving.

As other initiatives in this

> Having students make connections with one another can not only enhance students' experiences, but also assist the institution in retention efforts.

book have indicated, the University strives to get new freshmen connected to faculty, staff, programs, etc. However, one important opportunity for connection is to get students connected to each other. Having students make connections with one another can not only enhance students' experiences, but also assist the institution in retention efforts. Freshmen spend more time with each other than anyone else, thus the significant impact student-to-student connections can have on their satisfaction with the institution. A student who has made friends and acknowledges meaningful relationships has a stronger support network should an issue arise. Additionally, if the student is considering leaving the University, I am hopeful their positive experiences with their peers and the friendships they have made will influence them to remain enrolled. This would be in sharp contrast to a student who is considering leaving the University and who has unfavorable memories of experiences with his peers during the first year. That specific type of student would likely leave the institution with no regrets and no plans of ever returning. The more meaningful connections that freshmen can make during the first year will only benefit everyone involved. I am hopeful that as the University of Mississippi continues to grow, it never becomes too large where new students have trouble making connections during their first year on campus.

Initiatives to Get Students Connected to Each Other

One would think it would be easy for new students to connect with each other. Unfortunately, from my experience it seems each year we are made more aware of new freshmen who have trouble making connections with their peers. I have several thoughts as to why we are seeing an increase in the number of cases: (a) The significant rise in the number of out-of-state freshmen, specifically those from long distances who come to the University without knowing anyone. These students may see other new freshmen who knew each other before their arrival and feel left out thinking every other new freshman already has a friend group. (b) Some of today's students have had most details of their lives planned out by their parents, thus they have never had to step outside their comfort zone. I have personally spoken to students who have told me their parents (usually the mother) controlled their lives. Their examples included where to work, what clubs to join, and who they could have as friends. The parent may have thought she was keeping the child safe and putting them on a path to success. However, once the parent dropped the student off at college and was no longer making the decisions, the student was lost and had trouble adapting. (c) Social media, cell phones, etc. have taken the place of personal face-to-face conversation for many of our students. When they are texting and interacting with friends back home, these students miss out on meeting new people on campus. Some may argue that technology has caused today's students to not know how to interact socially when trying to make new friends. Regardless of the reasons for why new freshmen may have trouble making connections with peers,

University professionals, who work with student success and retention understand it is important to help students overcome all barriers and get connected. At the University of Mississippi, there are several initiatives we utilize to help our new freshmen get connected to one another.

Summer Orientation

Every new student (freshman and transfer) is required to participate in Orientation. Orientations provide new students the opportunity to learn about academic and non-academic facets of the University. Freshman Orientation lasts two days. The first day is focused on the non-academic services and programs that new students may be exposed to during their time at the institution. Sessions about financial aid, getting involved, and respecting the institution are examples of the types of information that is discussed during the first day. Additionally, after dinner on the first night there is a campus organization browse fair where current students can interact with new students while discussing their respective organizations. On Day Two, new students attend an academic dean's meeting, meet with an academic advisor, and register for classes. Parents have separate informational sessions that occur during both days while their students are following the orientation schedule.

Students connect with each other while discussing fall classes during summer orientation.

As one can imagine, there are many opportunities for new students to connect with each other during the two-day event. Some of the connections happen organically, while other opportunities are pre-planned. New students sit by each other during informational sessions and during meals, and at other moments where natural conversations can occur and new friendships can be made. However, the primary way for new students to connect during Orientation is through their orientation leaders. Orientation leaders are current students who are hired and trained by the Office of Admis-

New freshmen participate in an ice breaker activity during Summer Orientation.

sions (Admissions oversees Orientation). Orientation Leaders are seen as a source of information, as well as peers who can relate to what new students are experiencing. Each Orientation Leader is responsible for a small group of about 15 students at each Orientation. Orientation leaders strive to get to know their group members while encouraging the new students to get to know each other. They coordinate ice- breaker activities, which allow students to interact. Additionally, there are scheduled meeting times that enable the Orientation Leader to lead a discussion that incorporates feedback from the group. This interaction provides the students the opportunity to connect to other new students so hopefully when they arrive for the fall semester, they will have a small group of friends already established. Furthermore, the Orientation leaders encourage new students to contact them with any questions or concerns once the fall semester is underway.

Although Day Two of Orientation is primarily focused on academics, there are several opportunities for students to connect. These connections usually revolve around a student's academic major. Following breakfast, students will sit next to each other during their academic dean's meeting. Before and after (and sometimes during) the deans' talks, students will chat about their majors, career plans, and have similar discussions, thus connections between like-minded individuals can occur. After the dean's meeting students will proceed to their assigned academic advisors. When students arrive at the advisor's office, they may have to wait while another new student is getting advised. Similar to a dean's meeting, while students are waiting, they have the opportunity to interact with peers who are interested in similar fields of study. The final opportunity for connections related to academics occurs after academic advising and students register for classes in computer labs. Many students will register for courses while sitting next to other new students who have a similar major. It is not uncommon for students to have conversations about course selection. Students may discuss certain professors they have heard about or how far the walk is from Point A to Point B. Ultimately, some of these students will register for the same sections of various courses. This academic connection allows new students to connect with at least one person in some of their courses. Because most new freshmen take a general core of classes during their first semester (e.g., Writing 1, Social Science, First-Year Experience, etc.) at the University, even students who do not have the same major, but sit next to each other in the computer lab may register for some of the same sections. Again, in the world of retention it is all about getting students connected. I'm grateful that Orientation provides the opportunity for both academic and non-academic connections to occur before the students officially begin their enrollment at the University of Mississippi.

Orientation provides the opportunity for both academic and non-academic connections before the students begin their enrollment at the University of Mississippi.

Students meeting each other while participating in Ballpit with strangers during Welcome Week

Welcome week activities

The first week of the fall semester always has a special buzz in the air. New students are excited, nervous, happy, sad, and every emotion in between. Many are away from home for the first time and are trying to navigate this new world known as higher education. After a few weeks the buzz will wear off as most students will have settled into a routine, made friends, and adapted to college life. However, the first week is critical in helping new students realize they made a great decision in choosing the University of Mississippi. Therefore, the University schedules several events during the first week to give students something to do and allows for connections to be made. Some of the events that occur during the first week, known as Welcome Week, include: Movie Night in the Grove, New Student Picnic and Pep Rally, Get Involved Fair, Fall Convocation, various department-sponsored activities, interactive events in front of the student union, and a concert in the Grove. All these events are free and provide new students the opportunity to engage with their peers while participating in educational and social events. Some of the connections made during the first week, while participating in the University's sponsored events, have the potential to lead to lifelong friendships or relationships. However, even if these connections do not last a lifetime, we are hopeful that enough students will begin a relationship, thus supporting our primary purpose of getting them connected to other freshmen so they feel comfortable and the chances of persistence increase.

Below are brief descriptions of some of the events that occur during Welcome Week:

Movie Night in the Grove: Movie Night usually occurs on the Friday night before the fall semester begins on Monday. Students are informed of this event through a variety of avenues, including fliers in the residence halls during move-in. Additionally, some professional staff members in the Department of Student Housing may promote the event and encourage new students to walk to the venue together and enjoy the movie. Whether students meet in a residence hall and walk over or get acquainted once they are sitting in the Grove, the opportunity to interact and connect with other new freshmen is ever-present.

New Student Picnic and Pep Rally: The picnic and pep rally is held on the Saturday before the semester begins. New freshmen attend residence hall floor meetings and then walk to the Grove together. I appreciate the meetings that occur beforehand, as they allow residents to meet each other and enjoy a new group of friends with which to attend the picnic. Food and drinks are served at the event followed by the band and cheerleaders leading a pep rally. Occasionally, the athletic director, football coach, and/or football players speak. Many Student Affairs staff attend in an effort to make students feel welcome. Hosting an informal social event such as a picnic allows students the ability to move around while interacting with new classmates.

Get Involved Fair: This event usually occurs midday on Tuesday and Wednesday during the first week of classes. The fair allows representatives from student organizations to encourage students to discuss their organization. New students find this casual, yet informative, setting ideal as they learn about the numerous organizations and ways to get involved on campus. New students have the opportunity to get connected to current students, their organization, and potentially, other new students who have similar interests.

Fall Convocation: Fall Convocation is an opportunity for all new freshmen to be welcomed to campus by senior administrators, and to hear a reading and presentation by the author of the common reading selection. Freshmen who are enrolled in EDHE 105 are required to attend so some classes choose to meet in a specific location and walk to the venue together. Each dean is introduced so new students can become familiar with the one who represents their school or college. Additionally, the provost and chancellor welcome the new students and present each student with a class coin. When issuing the coins, students are challenged to keep the coin and bring it with them four years later when they cross the stage at graduation. Although convocation is a formal academic event, students have the opportunity to see many of their new peers in one location. An event like this will not happen again until graduation. I am hopeful this common experience allows for connections to be made.

Department-hosted activities: During Welcome Week various departments host events on campus. The Center for Inclusion and Cross Cultural Engagement, for example, may host a cookout and open house. The Department of Campus Recreation usually hosts a Late Night with Campus Recreation where students can play games and win prizes. Additionally, the late night event keeps students on campus and gives them a way to participate in something fun and active. These casual social events are perfect for new students to find other new students who share similar interests.

Interactive events in front of the Student Union: The Student Union is seen as a meeting place for many students on campus. It is conveniently located next to the Grove and houses the bookstore, food court, and other amenities that provide students a reason to gather. Therefore, it is no coincidence that Welcome Week features many smaller events, daily, that are held in front of the Student Union. One day, free ice cream may be passed out while live music plays in the background.

On another day, Ball Pit with Strangers, an event aimed at getting new students to meet others, may be held. Students volunteer to get into a ball pit that has enough room for three or four students. No one in the group should know each other beforehand so during the time they are in the ball pit together, they are meeting new people. Whether it is playing laser tag in the Grove or meeting new people in a ball pit, the small events in front of the Student Union during Welcome Week provide students with an opportunity to connect with their peers.

Concert in the Grove: One of the highlights of Welcome Week occurs at the end of the week when there is a free outdoor concert in the Grove. Over the years the acts have ranged from popular performers to up-and-coming stars. Regardless of the type of music, the Grove is always packed for the concert. This finale provides a great venue for students to enjoy entertainment with their friends. The outdoor concert provides a very relaxed atmosphere where students can hear the music, yet still engage in conversation.

First-Year Experience Course

The first-year experience course at the University of Mississippi has been frequently mentioned throughout this book. The course provides an excellent opportunity to support our new freshmen while assisting them in connecting to the instructor, their major, campus resources, and the institution. However, the components of the course, as well as the instructor, are able to offer the students the ability to connect with each other while participating in activities and lessons. Unlike traditional lecture-based courses where a professor does a majority of the speaking, EDHE 105 is designed to encourage class discussion. Many book chapters feature important information while posing open-ended questions that allow the students to express their opinions on various topics. For example, the chapter on wellness may lead to a conversation about how individual students remain healthy while in college. This open dialogue allows students to identify with others in the course, thus potentially assisting them to find commonalities and make connections with like-minded peers.

Outside-of-class assignments and programs also can lead to students making connections with their classmates. Many of the sections use an activity known as a photo scavenger hunt. The instructor will randomly select small groups of students to visit important places on campus and take a group photo at the location. Locations are pertinent to students and may include: Student Health Center, Office of Financial Aid, Turner Center (Campus Recreation), and other places that are important to students. Once all the sites have been visited one group member e-mails all pictures to the instructor. The instructor will then show all group pictures in class. The more creative groups are with their pictures, the more the class seems to enjoy the assignment. This activity allows for students to learn important locations and forces them to get to know other class members. Ideally, this assignment is given early in the semester.

Outside-of-class programs also are conducive to helping students connect with each other. Although there are some programs that are required of all sections (e.g., active shooter presentations by the University Police Department, library presentations, etc.) others vary by instructor. Some may choose to host educational events, such as a campus historical tour or a walk to William Faulkner's home at Rowan Oak; while others may choose more social or active activities like a group exercise class provide by the Department of Campus Recreation or a visit to the ropes course. Regardless of the event, class members will participate in a shared experience that encourages them to reflect and share their opinions. These opportunities allow participants to learn about each other in ways that a standard class lecture, where the professor speaks and the students take notes, would not. Overall, the EDHE 105 course is an excellent tool for student-to-student connections to occur.

Regional/state meet and greets

For years the Academic Support Center (now the Center for Student Success and First-Year Experience) hosted meet-and-greets for new freshmen based on their academic major. Although we understood how important it was for freshmen to make a connection to their major and/or faculty representing their department, student attendance was poor, regardless of our efforts to promote the event. We began partnering with the first-year experience course to promote the event. Some instructors required their students to attend, while others awarded extra credit; unfortunately, there were a few who chose not to mention it to their classes. This partnership immediately increased attendance. However, based on feedback from students and department representatives, limited connections were made and most felt it was a waste of their time. Therefore, we discontinued the event based on academic major and restructured it to be more conducive with our retention goals.

Every year we lose freshmen who cite "distance from home" or "social fit" as their primary reason for departure. To combat this problem, the Center for Student Success and First-Year Experience (CSSFYE) decided to host informal meet-and-greets based on geographic location. Using data to determine the home residencies of students who cited the two aforementioned reasons for leaving, in 2015 the CSSFYE hosted seven regional/state events for new freshmen. In my opinion, the inaugural year of this initiative yielded good, but not great, results. With over 50% of the freshmen class being non-residents, this initiative made perfect sense as a way to get new students connected. I was especially excited for the meet-and-greets that would connect students who were far from home and were experiencing Ole Miss/Mississippi/the South for the first time. Although some students may have come for a football game or a campus visit while exploring their college options, there is definitely an adjustment to living in Oxford, Mississippi for new students hailing from areas such as New York, Los Angeles, Chicago, etc.

The regional/state meet and greets occurred during weeks two and three of the fall semester. Each event was held at 5 p.m. and lasted one hour. Our hope was that students would connect with each other then go to dinner together and continue their conversations. Approximately 100-150 new freshmen from specific states/regions were invited to each event. States that could support 100-150 students on their own (e.g., Florida, Illinois, and Missouri), sponsored their own event. Other states that did not have enough new freshmen were grouped together by region (e.g., East Coast, Northeast, Midwest, West Coast). Although I was hopeful for at least 50 new freshmen at each event, we did not achieve that number at any event. The West Coast, Northeast, and Illinois events were the largest, with approximately 30 attendees. The East Coast was the smallest with less than 10 in attendance. We did not offer similar events for Mississippi residents, states bordering Mississippi, or Georgia or Texas (which both claimed more than 300 University freshmen) because our metrics did not identify an urgent need to target these groups. Although attendance was not as robust as I had originally hoped, the students who did attend, as well as the staff members who hosted the event, provided positive feedback. The CSSFYE learned a lot during the inaugural year and plans to host these events for new freshmen during the upcoming fall semester. The opportunity for these new students to connect with others who have a natural commonality – home state or region – is apparent, so continual improvement on this initiative should help with overall freshman retention.

Staff members assisting with connections

University faculty, staff, and administrators (specifically, those directly involved in retention efforts) understand how important it is for new students to make connections during the first year. It is not uncommon for campus professionals to be made aware of students who are struggling to find their niche at the University. When this occurs, the employee usually makes students aware of ways to get involved on campus, refers the student to another campus professional, and is occasionally able to directly connect the student to a peer, who shares a commonality. For the purpose of this section, I will share a few ideas related to the how campus professionals can help students get connected.

During the 2014-15 academic year, the mother of a freshman contacted me, concerned that her son was unhappy and wanted to transfer. After speaking with her, I discovered that her son did not participate in Greek Life, while many of the friends he made during the first few weeks of the semester chose to join a fraternity. The student felt like he had lost his support group and wanted to transfer to a school closer to home that many of his high school friends chose to attend. I convinced the student to meet with me. After getting to know him, I suggested several ways he could get involved on campus that were based on his interests. Although I made referrals, I also knew another freshman who had similar interests and who also chose not to participate in Greek Life. This student was in my EDHE 105 class, so I had a prior relationship with him. After gaining the student's permission to contact the other student, I talked with my former EDHE 105 student. He was more than willing to share his contact information. In my mind I was confident these two could be friends because they were both non-residents, did not participate in Greek Life, and enjoyed sports and exercising. After I provided each student with the other's contact information, I waited a few weeks before touching base with the student from my EDHE 105 class. Fortunately, I was correct in my assumptions, as the two became friends, who regularly exercised together and generally, hung out. Additionally, I found out they lived in the same residence hall (something I previously did not know), and they joined an intramural team that won their league. I was pleased that his example had a happy ending for the student, and equally gratified that our retention rate did not take a hit.

Another recent example also involves a freshman from the 2014 cohort. Similar to the student in my first example, a mother contacted me (further proof it is good to partner with parents during the first year), stating her daughter was unhappy and wanted to transfer to a school closer to home. This student also chose not to participate in Greek Life and felt isolated when many of the females in her residence hall chose to join a sorority. I met with this student and attempted to learn more about her and help her get connected. She was very passionate about a specific interest, but unfortunately, we had no student organizations related to her specific pursuit. Although, I brainstormed ways that she could still be engaged with her passion, nothing directly on campus was able to connect. This out-of-state student was far from home. Fortunately, I had another female in my EDHE 101 class who hailed from the same state. As you may recall, EDHE 101 is for students on academic probation. I was a little hesitant at first about offering to connect them, as the first student had almost a 4.0, while the other student was on academic probation. I was unsure if their approach to academics would indicate incompatibility. Still, I decided to try to connect them. Both girls agreed to receive the other's contact information. Several weeks went by before the mother of the first student contacted me with an unrelated question. In my response, I inquired about how the student was doing after our meeting. The mother said things had greatly improved and that the two students were now very good friends. After receiving this information, I spoke with the student in my EDHE 101 class. It turns out that she was also feeling homesick, so the two naturally connected. Since this scenario occurred two years ago, I do have some follow-up. The student who expressed the desire to leave the University not only ended up staying, but was hired for an on-campus job in which she interacts with current freshmen. I am hopeful her experience of overcoming the feeling of isolation can help her encourage other new freshmen who share the same feelings. Additionally, because the University did not have a student organization that supported her specific interest, she ended up starting her own club, which now has about 40 members and is occasionally mentioned in various campus news outlets. Ultimately, I am truly pleased that both students were not only retained, but strengthened by the connections that helped them enjoy their time as undergraduate students.

Student to student connections are essential in successful retention efforts.

Connecting Students to Each Other

Think about your current efforts to assist students in getting connected to their peers.

Who are the people/departments responsible?:

_____

_____

_____

_____

What types of connection attempts are coordinated?:

_____

_____

_____

_____

How does their connection efforts benefit freshman retention?:

_____

_____

_____

_____

Brainstorm ways to increase student-to-student connection efforts.

_____

_____

_____

_____

_____

_____

_____

Interview

Martin Fisher
Admissions Assistant Director-Orientation and Campus Visits

Describe your role in helping new freshmen make connections.

I have the privilege of directing new student orientation at the University of Mississippi. In that role, I help facilitate a day-and-a-half program that involves presentations from campus leaders, small group activities with peers, and much more. It is our hope that incoming freshmen will have the opportunity at orientation to connect with peers, current student leaders, faculty/staff, and potential student organizations to join.

In your opinion, what are some of the most effective connection strategies at the University?

I may be a bit biased, but I truly believe orientation is one of the most effective connection strategies our University offers. When training orientation leaders, we put a huge emphasis on how we want to make new students feel when they attend orientation. Many students come to orientation a bit unsure of their college choice or hesitant because they do not know anyone else attending Ole Miss. Our orientation leaders are intentional in their interactions with those students.

One of the first activities we do at orientation is break the students into small groups of 15-20 with one orientation leader, and they participate in icebreakers and get to know each other. Students spend most of the first day with their small group. These connections give students a sense of stability as they prepare for their first semester at UM. In addition to connecting with their peers, new students have numerous opportunities to connect with administrators, faculty, and staff while they are on campus for orientation. Our goal is for students to have connections made before the semester begins that will make them successful in and out of the classroom.

Since you became involved in the University's Orientation Program, describe some changes related to helping new students get connected you have observed.

We reformatted our schedule on day 1 of orientation to separate students from their family members who are here with them for orientation. After the first hour of the program, students are dismissed to their small groups and do not see their family members until dinner. This programming forces students to interact with their peers and presenters instead of relying on the comfort of sitting with their family. Another programmatic change we have made is the timing of the Get Involved presentation and Rebel Roundup. The last presentation students hear on day 1 is about how to get involved on campus. Student leaders and representatives from the Office of the Dean of Students discuss the importance of engaging in campus life outside of the classroom. As soon as they finish that presentation, students have the opportunity to network with registered student organizations in a browse fair format called Rebel Roundup.

Where do you see connection efforts going in the short term? Long term?

In the short-term, I hope to continue to add more elements to our orientation social called "Hotty Toddy Hangout". We added quite a few games this year that gave students more opportunities to meet new friends and network with each other in a safe environment. A long-term goal is to seek ways to individualize and improve the connections made during the advising/course registration process.

What advice would you give other institutions regarding helping new students get connected?

My advice is to not over program. Some of our most fruitful times at orientation are during free time or other less formal opportunities for students to connect with one another and the campus community as a whole.

INITIATIVE 15
PROFESSIONAL DEVELOPMENT/BEST PRACTICES

The University of Mississippi strives to promote and encourage continuous professional development and the utilization of best practices. Whether faculty, staff, and administrators engage in professional development on or off-campus, continuing to grow one's knowledge is paramount in efficient and effective student support services. Based on my personal experience, being engaged in various professional development opportunities and understanding best practices in specific areas has helped our retention efforts at the University of Mississippi. This initiative will provide information and examples of ways the University and I have benefited from participating in professional development and implementing best practices. I am confident many of the retention professionals who are reading this book already value professional development and will utilize the information provided in this initiative to further validate that they are making wise decisions when choosing to participate in growth opportunities.

Importance of Professional Development

Regardless of one's job title or campus department, participating in professional development has numerous benefits. Professional development opportunities can help faculty, staff, and administrators, expand knowledge, increase skills, and make connections to colleagues from other institutions who have similar interests. Furthermore, participating in professional development has never been easier, as almost every aspect of higher education has a professional association that delivers content to appropriate clientele. If you have read the previous 14 initiatives, I trust you understand that retention is an "all hands on deck" effort. Therefore, professionals from across campus can make an impact on retention in a variety of ways. With this important factor in mind, understand that most of the people involved in retention efforts have a professional association and other professional development opportunities available, which can help guide their practice as it relates to helping students persist.

Many of the professional associations in which I have been involved over the last 12 years have conferences with presenta-

Professional development opportunities can help faculty, staff, and administrators expand knowledge, increase skills, and make connections to colleagues from other institutions who have similar interests.

tions, consultations, webinars, journals, books, etc. that focus on student retention as it relates to that specific association's mission. Based on conversations with University colleagues, who are involved with our retention efforts, their associations also offer information, resources, and guidance regarding student retention to their membership. From professional associations related to student housing, financial aid, and even orientation, retention is a hot topic that is frequently discussed. Having campus partners, who are involved in retention efforts and who participate in professional development, can be a valuable asset in student persistence. Retention benefits can occur when people participate in development opportunities both on and off campus. For example, if a staff member from the Department of Student Housing attends a professional association conference related to housing and gains new insight regarding learning communities' role in retention, that person's new insight could directly benefit our student support efforts. Additionally, if that staff member then gave a presentation on learning communities at a campus academic advising luncheon, a faculty member may gain interest in this concept and approach the Department of Student Housing about a new learning community where that faculty member could be the advisor and serve students. In that example, learning occurred off-campus through the professional association, but the ripple effect allowed learning to occur on-campus, thus potentially doubling our ability to support and retain students.

I have been actively involved in many professional development opportunities since I began at the University in 2004. By furthering my education, participating in professional associations and on-campus programs, I have welcomed the opportunity to grow as a professional in higher education. This continued development has served me well in my work with freshman retention. When I first began as an academic advisor, I did not realize the level of importance that student retention was to institutions of higher learning. Fortunately, as my knowledge, skills, and education evolved, I was fully capable to help lead efforts aligned with the

University making retention a priority. One of the associations I joined early in my career focused on supporting the work of academic advisors. I am still involved with this association, but my areas of interest within the association have changed. Now I focus on publications, and presentations from the association that highlight retention. Fortunately, with retention being a hot topic, this association provides an ample amount of information. In the past there were not very many presentations at conferences related to academic advisors' roles in retention. However, that has changed over the years. Now there are numerous sessions that provide information related to how quality academic advising can impact retention. I appreciate the opportunity to learn what other colleagues are doing and the ability to bring ideas back to my campus for discussion and possible implementation.

In addition to gaining new knowledge, the professional association helped me acquire several mentors, as well as a vast network of colleagues who can offer insight to any issue. These relationships have been very beneficial. The more experienced advisors and administrators who took me under their wings were a great resource as I grew in the association and profession. Many of the lessons and guidance I received from these mentors are still put to use in my daily work. The network of colleagues I have today also is an important benefit to being involved in the professional association. When an issue, question, or potential new initiative arises, I know I have several colleagues from across the country who can provide assistance. Furthermore, these higher education professionals know they can contact me for assistance. I encourage everyone who works in student success and retention to develop a network of colleagues who can provide guidance when needed. Although professional associations are known for the content they provide members, the opportunities to expand one's network must not be overlooked.

IMPORTANCE OF BEST PRACTICES

While professional development is important for individuals and the programs in which they interact, the utilization of best practices is equally as important. These two concepts can go hand-in-hand with the winners being the campus professionals, students, and the institution. It is not uncommon for campus members to learn about best practices while engaging in professional development. Understanding best practices is important in order to keep retention efforts current and to maximize opportunities. The University of Mississippi has benefited over the years from exploring other institutions' best practices and fully implementing, revising, or discussing programs and initiatives that have worked well elsewhere.

> Understanding best practices is important in order to keep retention efforts current and to maximize opportunities.

I can recall several best practices from other institutions that we have adapted to fit the needs of our students. One of the best examples that has benefited our institution is a program from the Georgia Institute of Technology (Georgia Tech). Several years ago, while attending a regional academic advising conference, I attended a presentation by Georgia Tech staff members regarding their on-campus academic advising network. Fortunately, on the plane ride home I sat next to our associate provost, who was open to the idea of creating an on-campus academic advising network at our institution. The next year, using some of Georgia Tech's concepts and adding our own, the University of Mississippi developed the Ole Miss Academic Advising Network (OMANN). The implementation of this best practice has been an asset in sharing advising information, professional development, and many other benefits to the University's advising community. Another great example of implementing a best practice is our first-year experience course. The University had a similar course in year's past, but it was not well received and was eventually discontinued. When the University began to take a serious look at freshman retention, one recommendation was that we revive our first-year experience course. However, we knew we could not bring it back under the same form. A small task force spent time looking at best practices from other institutions' first-year experience courses before submitting a proposal to reinstate the course with modifications. Modifications included making the course optional (previous offering was mandatory), allowing it to be worth three credit hours of general elective credit (previous offering was only one credit hour), and mandating that it be letter-graded (previous offering was only pass/fail). Today's course produces tremendous outcomes and is extremely valuable in our retention efforts. Although the course is frequently revised based on assessment, the general structure is very similar to what was created based on our knowledge of other institutions' best practices. Additional best practices that the University has utilized in some capacity include the use of professional academic advisors for freshmen, living and learning communities, a common reading experience, and other successful initiatives that our peers have found to be effective.

Regarding implementing best practices, I feel it is important to note that we have reciprocated so others can benefit. Over the last several years, numerous colleagues have informed me that they have implemented a variation of one or more of our programs/services after hearing about the University's success. University of Mississippi faculty, staff, and administrators (myself included) are proud of what we have achieved and do not mind sharing with our colleagues in higher education. It seems after almost every presentation, publication, and speaking engagement, I hear from colleagues who are attempting to implement something that has worked well for us, or who have additional questions before proposing implementation. Personally, I appreciate campus professionals from other institutions who are attempting to replicate something that has worked well for the University of Mississippi. I realize we have benefited from peer institutions' best practices, and there is no reason for others not to follow our path. After raising our retention rate by 8%, I have gone through the trial-and-error process that other institutions may experience, and am happy to share my perspective just as other colleagues have done with me.

OMAAN Luncheons draw a diverse crowd of faculty, professional, and advising administrators from across campus.

Professional Development at the University of Mississippi

As previously mentioned, there is a lot to learn from off-campus professional development opportunities. However, there are numerous beneficial and cost-effective ways to engage in professional development on-campus. By hosting on-campus events you are able to provide valuable information to a targeted audience. Additionally, the messages can be specific to fit a current issue that your campus is facing, while terminology and examples used will be easily recognized by attendees. Unlike attending a presentation at a large conference, hosting on-campus professional development events ensures that attendees will find the topics tailored to their areas of oversight. Furthermore, on-campus events have the ability to attract a large audience as costs, time away from work, and other issues are not factors for attendees. Below are some examples of on-campus professional development which I have been involved. Many of these opportunities are directly related to our retention efforts.

Weekly staff meeting

In every office I have worked, we have had weekly staff meetings. These meetings usually consisted of the dissemination of information that directly affected our work. I admit that when I first began as an administrator, my meetings followed a similar format. However, I realized by having a captive audience of front-line retention professionals listening to me speak every week, there were opportunities to do more than provide work-related information. In our new weekly meeting structure, we spend the first half talking about issues pertaining to day-to-day operations. During the second half of the meeting someone is assigned to lead a professional development conversation. We use a rotation so each staff member will lead the conversation once every four months. Ideally, the person who leads will send all staff members an article, presentation or book excerpt a few days prior to the meeting. We have had great conversations and the staff seems to enjoy freely discussing pertinent issues during our meetings. Some of our topics have included: academic advisors' role in retention, parent involvement, finding joy in the workplace, supporting transfer students, and many others that provided great discussion and afforded our staff some professional development from the comfort of the conference room. I realize I am not alone on my campus in utilizing this cost-efficient opportunity to help staff members grow and develop. I am aware of other offices that do something similar during staff meetings. Additionally, I have been invited to speak to colleagues during their meetings. Extending an invitation to guests to speak at our meetings is something I am considering for the future.

Community of practice meetings

I am a member of the Wellness and Student Success Community of Practice. This community consists of the directors from Campus Recreation, Counseling Center, Career Center, Student Health, Student Disability Services, and Center for Student Success and First-Year Experience (me). Each member of this community reports to the assistant vice chancellor for student affairs. The Wellness and Student Success Community of Practice meets monthly. When this community first began meeting we would discuss what was happening in our departments, as well as items of interest for the entire group. However, in 2015 the community added a professional development component. Our professional development opportunities have come in two forms, where: (a) each member presents on various topics of interest; and (b) guest speakers discuss relevant items that affect everyone in the community.

The member presentations have been very useful, as we share many commonalities which presenters understand and can tailor presentations to suit our needs. An additional component to the presentations is that they are hosted in the home department of the presenter. The community set up a rotation where each member would host the monthly meeting when it was her turn to present. Under this model, not only did attendees increase their knowledge through presentation information, they also gained a better understanding of the host department's functions, staff, and location. Even though I knew each individual within the community, seeing all aspects of their space and gaining additional knowledge of services and programs, has helped me be a more informed campus professional. Although our presentation topics focus on our areas of oversight, they have over-arching educational opportunity attainment that can benefit all members. For example, the director of the Career Center shared with us outcomes that employers want to see in newly hired employees. With permissions from the presenter, I shared that information with my freshmen taking EDHE 105, graduate students enrolled in a course I co-teach, as well as my staff. The opportunity to share information that may not be directly related to one's direct area of oversight with fellow staff members is a great way to offer professional development.

Inviting guests from other areas of campus has also tremendously benefited our community of practice. The assistant vice chancellor for student affairs schedules the guest speakers and takes our suggestions under consideration. Most of our speakers are upper-level administrators whom we would not normally interact with daily, but are impacted by their work. For example, we had the vice chancellor for administration and finance attend one of our meetings. This person was very informative and answered questions from the group. Several topics were addressed such as the University's financial model, the importance of recruiting and retaining students in relation to tuition dollars, and how funding considerations are made. Although I can only control my department's budget, understanding how the finances worked for the entire institution was enlightening. Furthermore, hearing affirmation from the top financial administrator about the importance of our retention efforts was encouraging. Another guest who provided useful information was the director of Facilities Planning. The University of Mississippi has construction projects occurring all over campus. In fact, at the time of this publication, several of our community members have renovation and/or new building projects happening. This guest speaker gave us an update on all current and future projects. Not only was this valuable information to share with our staffs, we could also inform current and prospective students and families how new projects may benefit them. Each guest who has attended our meetings has been very professional and offered first-hand insight into facets of the University that will affect each of us. I highly recommend exploring professional development opportunities that could occur within a small group of campus professionals who share similar areas of oversight.

Other on-campus opportunities

The previously mentioned on-campus professional development opportunities are two for which I have personally been involved and can attest to their benefits. However, there are other campus opportunities that are cost effective, informative, and have the potential to help the University's retention efforts. Some examples include monthly events such as the Academic Advising Network, Student Affairs workshops, EDHE 105 instructor professional development, and annual events, such as the Student Affairs Professional Development Conference and the Student Grit and Resilience Summit. Although I have been occasionally involved with several of these events, they reach a broader audience as the topics vary from meeting to meeting. The Academic Advising Network will release the meeting topics at the beginning of the fall semester. This allows for professionals from across campus to pick the meetings that will be most beneficial to them. A meeting where the topic focuses on advising for study abroad may only draw advisors and administrators who are involved with programs or majors that have students opting to study out of the country. However, other topics such as advising student athletes, partnering with the Career Center, or advising students of color may attract a different group of advisors. Student Affairs workshops and EDHE 105 instructor professional development are similar in that a variety of topics are covered in order to provide opportunities to a wide array of campus professionals. The annual professional development events on our campus are more comprehensive in that they are only offered once a year so they last an entire day and cover several topics. Whether professionals on our campus opt to attend monthly meetings, annual events, or a combination, they are receiving valuable professional development that can impact their work at the University. In turn, their work has the potential to impact our retention efforts in a variety of ways. I am grateful the University of Mississippi affords so many on-campus opportunities for professional development.

Professional Organizations

As previously mentioned in this initiative, professional associations are extremely beneficial to the growth and development of faculty, staff, and administrators. Higher education professionals who are involved in retention efforts can gain valuable insight from professional associations through reading publications, attending conferences, and networking with colleagues. Additionally, one can share his expertise through a professional association by writing, presenting, and conversing with peers from other institutions. Since my role in freshman retention increased at the University, I shifted my focus to exploring this topic through a variety of professional associations. Listed below are some of the professional associations in which I have been involved and how I used their resources to improve my work at retention or share my knowledge with other higher education professionals:

National Academic Advising Association (NACADA): I have been involved in NACADA for many years. From attending numerous conferences to holding leadership positions, I have benefited tremendously from my experience with this professional association. From a retention perspective, I believe I have given as much as I have received. When attending conferences or reading the NACADA journal, I tend to focus on sessions and articles related to student retention. Some of these growth opportunities directly related to retention include: academic advisors' roles in supporting first-generation students, how to engage faculty advisors in retention efforts, and supporting student-veterans. Within the last five years my work with student success and retention has allowed me to provide insight to my peers. I published an article in the NACADA Journal that addressed the needs of freshmen who are undeclared in their majors. Additionally, I presented at three different NACADA Conferences covering topics such as conducting qualitative research in academic advising, NACADA's Emerging Leader Program, and writing for NACADA.

National Resource Center (NRC) First-Year Experience and Students in Transition: My involvement with the NRC has not been as extensive as my work with NACADA. However, this group provides a wealth of information and opportunities for campus professionals who work with first-year students (freshmen and transfers). Although my time working with this group has been minimal, I have benefited from attending two of their conferences over the last two years. The presentations were valuable, covering topics such as early alert intervention, assessing your first-year experience course, and supporting freshmen on academic probation. Additionally, I spent an afternoon in a pre-conference workshop designed to inform attendees on the best ways to support transfer students. The presentations were very informative, but some of the best information I obtained was from casual networking while at the conference. I have been pleased with the services of the NRC and recently submitted a presentation proposal for an upcoming conference.

Student Affairs Administrators in Higher Education (NASPA): Similar to the NRC, my involvement in NASPA has only recently increased. For the first nine years of my career in higher education, I was under academic affairs. However, after the Center of Student Success and First-Year Experience was created in 2013, I began reporting to the Division of Student Affairs. NASPA has been a valuable resource to me, as the association is very comprehensive, much like our freshman retention efforts. I have attended two of their conferences and even presented at the 2015 event held in New Orleans. Although a NASPA conference is much larger than some of the other professional association conferences, I have found it easy to get connected to colleagues at other institutions who have similar interests. The casual networking during, and the after-conference follow-up, have been valuable. Sessions have offered exploring retention through a variety of perspectives. I have attended sessions on retaining students through the use of learning communities, student affairs and academic affairs collaborations in support of retention, and studying grit and resiliency among college students (definitely a retention issue). Furthermore, the presentation we gave in New Orleans regarding our successful first-year experience course highlighted the role it plays in our retention efforts.

Consortium on Student Retention Data Exchange (CSRDE): The CSRDE is a group I was unfamiliar with until freshman retention became a focal point of my job. I have quickly learned that the CSRDE is one of the "go to" resources for anything and everything related to student retention. Although other associations focus on retention in various capacities, the CSRDE is 100% committed to supporting professionals who work in student persistence. In my early years of involvement with the CSRDE, I simply attended conferences, attended sessions, networked with colleagues, and learned as much as possible. However, within the past several years I have published, given presentations, and presented a webinar for the CSRDE. I encourage higher education professionals, who work in student retention, to consider exploring the CSRDE's professional development opportunities, as all conferences, webinars, and networking focus on student persistence.

UM campus professionals after receiving a national award from NACADA.

Professional Development/Best Practices

Do you believe your institution currently supports professional development and the utilization of best practices?

What types of professional development opportunities are offered for employees on your campus:

What types of best practices are utilized on your campus?:

How does continued professional development and the utilization of best practices impact your freshman retention efforts?:

Brainstorm ways to increase opportunities for professional development and/or the utilization of best practices.

Interview

Dr. Patrick Perry
Director or Luckyday programs

Describe your role in the University's commitment to providing professional development and utilizing best practices.

I work primarily to coordinate professional development for instructors of EDHE105 (The First Year Experience Course) and EDHE305 (The Transfer Year Experience Course). In the past three years we have developed a model of professional development reflecting many best practices used at other institutions but adapted to fit the needs and culture of the University of Mississippi. I also participate by presenting professional development programs on emotional intelligence and grit and resiliency.

In your opinion, what are some of the most effective professional development opportunities at the University?

I believe that the most effective professional development opportunities on our campus involve partnerships between academic and student affairs. Literature on first year experience programs speaks to the fact that a strong partnership between academic and student affairs is critical to being fully successful. As an example, although the Center for Student Success and First-Year Experience (CSSFYE) is housed under the Division of Student Affairs, there is significant support and partnerships with faculty in education, history, English, writing and rhetoric, psychology and other academic disciplines.

Since you became involved in the University's promotion of professional development, describe some changes you have observed.

In the past few years I have noticed the strengthening of the partnership between academic and student affairs. All first-year success stakeholders are coming together more and more to share in the dialogue on how to better serve our first year students.

Where do you see professional development opportunities going in the short term? Long term?

I believe that in the short term much of the professional development has shifted recently towards development of non-cognitive skills such as impulse control, decision-making, grit, interpersonal relationships. In the last two decades, universities have significantly increased the academic support structures students have access to on their campuses. First-Year support centers and classes, Supplemental Instruction, Tutoring Opportunities and other academic success focused initiatives seem available to most students attending college. In recent years there has been a shift to not only meet the academic needs of our students but also to be proactive with the non-academic needs mentioned above. Long term I also believe much professional development will be online via learning modules and assessments will be used to validate proficiency by instructors.

What advice would you give other institutions regarding their professional development opportunities and the utilization of best practices?

1. Make it fun
2. Make sure it is organized
3. Realize you will not be able to please all stakeholders so do the best you are able and try to get input from everyone involved
4. Provide incentives (monetary, door prizes, certifications, etc.)
5. Connect with tenure process (not sure if this is possible but could be a game changer)

CONCLUSION

When I began my career in higher education, I did not know what the future would hold. However, from day one to the present, there has been a constant motivator that drove me to work hard each and every day. That motivator was my desire to see students be successful in higher education. During my undergraduate and graduate days, I had several professionals who took an interest in my success. Although my career path in higher education has taken several turns, the genuine interest that was shown to me while pursuing degrees, was my driving force to assist other students to the best of my ability. This valuable outlook has been critical in our success at retaining our freshmen. I have learned many tips, tricks, and secrets throughout my time working in higher education. However, the one attribute a person who works in retention must have is the ability to genuinely care about each and every student.

This book highlighted 15 initiatives that have been essential in raising our freshman retention rate from 78% to over 86%. Each initiative is very important and many work in conjunction with one another. Over the last eight years in working with freshman retention, I have learned there is no easy answer or quick fix. I firmly believe our retention rates have drastically improved thanks to hard work, dedication, and support from numerous people across campus. Furthermore, the three most important lessons I have learned are: (a) treat every student as an individual; (b) have faculty, staff, and administrators who care about student success, satisfaction, and persistence; and (c) develop a retention culture on campus. Moving the retention needle is difficult, but with proper support and strategic efforts, it can be accomplished. I am hopeful this practitioner's guide has been useful to my higher education colleagues in their efforts to support and retain students.

ACKNOWLEDGMENTS

The most important people in my life are family. This book would not have been possible without them. My wife Laurie Beth, and sons Carson and Denton, have been very supportive throughout the duration of this project. They spent many weekend afternoons or evenings doing things without me to allow time for peaceful writing. My mother, Paula Spears, has been an asset from the start. Her encouragement during all of my academic pursuits has not gone unnoticed. I could not ask for better family support and this acknowledgment is a small token of my appreciation for them.

The team at Nautilus Publishing has been great. Neil White, Carroll Moore, and Sinclair Rishel were easy to work with and provided guidance and support throughout the process. They are very good at what they do and this book would not have been possible without them. While hearing Dr. Robert Khayat talk about his experience writing the book *The Education of a Lifetime*, he gave Neil and the team at Nautilus much of the credit. Furthermore, Dr. Khayat noted that anyone who is thinking about writing a book should have a conversation with Neil. I am grateful for his advice and happy I followed up with Neil.

I truly appreciate my colleagues and friends who are involved in retention efforts at the University of Mississippi. Many of these people provided interviews for the book. Without their hard work and dedication, the University's retention rates would not have seen such a significant increase, thus this book would not exist. Additionally, I am greatly indebted to the hundreds of front line campus professionals who work daily in student success and persistence. Academic advisors, EDHE instructors, Financial Aid staff, Student Housing professionals and others on campus have been instrumental in the University's success. These front line heroes make the retention magic happen!

I would like to thank several individuals who have directly contributed to this book. Deidra Jackson was the first person to proof my initial draft. I appreciate her editing content and offering suggestions which strengthened my work. I am grateful for Ken Sufka —University of Mississippi, John Paul Regalado —University of Texas A&M Corpus Christi, Kathleen Smith — University of Oklahoma, and Sandra Whalen — Consortium for Student Retention Data Exchange (CSRDE) who all agreed to read the book prior to its release and offer their feedback. These people are very well respected in higher education and their support reaffirms how valuable our work is to student success, satisfaction, and persistence. Finally, I could not have asked for a better person than Joe Cuseo to write the foreword for this book. Joe is a rock star in the world of student success and his work has lead to many innovations on our campus. From his consulting visits to campus, catching up at conferences, and personal communication, Joe has not only influenced my work in higher education, he has assisted the University of Mississippi in transforming how we serve our students.

Made in the USA
Middletown, DE
07 June 2017